OpenStack Administration with Ansible

Design, build, and automate 10 real-world OpenStack administrative tasks with Ansible

Walter Bentley

PUBLISHING

BIRMINGHAM - MUMBAI

OpenStack Administration with Ansible

First published: January 2016

Production reference: 1210116

Published by Packt Publishing Ltd.
Livery Place
35 Livery Street
Birmingham B3 2PB, UK.

ISBN 978-1-78588-461-0

www.packtpub.com

Credits

Author
Walter Bentley

Reviewer
Diego Woitasen

Commissioning Editor
Veena Pagare

Acquisition Editor
Meeta Rajani

Content Development Editor
Susmita Sabat

Technical Editor
Madhunikita Sunil Chindarkar

Copy Editor
Sneha Singh

Project Coordinator
Milton Dsouza

Proofreader
Safis Editing

Indexer
Hemangini Bari

Production Coordinator
Shantanu N. Zagade

Cover Work
Shantanu N. Zagade

About the Author

Walter Bentley is a private cloud solutions architect with Rackspace. He has a diverse background in production systems administration and solutions architecture. He has over 15 years of experience across numerous industries, such as online marketing, finance, insurance, aviation, food, education, and now in technology product space. In the past, he has typically been the requestor, consumer, and advisor to companies in the use of technologies such as OpenStack. He is now a promoter of OpenStack technology and a cloud educator.

In Walter's current role, he is focused on helping customers build, design, and deploy private clouds built on OpenStack. His role also involves professional services, engagements around operating the built OpenStack clouds, and DevOps engagements creating playbooks/roles with Ansible.

Recently, Walter was given the honor to be present at the OpenStack Vancouver and Tokyo Summits. As well as this, he was given the great opportunity to present at AnsibleFest events in London and New York. Some of his other experiences involve performing webinars, blogging about OpenStack, and speaking at various technology conferences. Another wonderful experience is Walter being allowed to take part in the technical review of the newly launched *OpenStack Cloud Computing Cookbook, Third Edition, Packt Publishing*.

Acknowledgments

I would like to thank my wife and best friend, Tasha, for allowing me to take on this life-changing opportunity; I don't think it would have been possible without her understanding and support. She is truly my life's motivation. Also, I wish to thank my wonderful daughters, London and Rio, for bringing so much joy to our lives. I would like to thank my mother and father for cultivating the technical spirit within me from a very early age (that Commodore 64 was definitely my springboard… LOL).

I would also like to thank my coworker and fellow architect Kevin Jackson, for providing me with the courage to take on this project. I also wish to say thanks and express my gratitude to all of my mentors over the years that I have had the privilege to work for; those individuals include David Bartlett, Tyrone Paige, Steve Contrabasso, and Mike Childress. Their multitude of great advice has allowed me to be where I am today.

About the Reviewer

Diego Woitasen has more than 10 years of experience in the Linux and open source consulting industry. He is (with Luis Vinay) the co-founder of `http://flugel.it/`, self-denominated infrastructure developers; they apply all those years of experience to help all sorts of companies to embrace the DevOps culture and the new movements related with interdisciplinary cooperative working environments.

www.PacktPub.com

Support files, eBooks, discount offers, and more

For support files and downloads related to your book, please visit www.PacktPub.com.

Did you know that Packt offers eBook versions of every book published, with PDF and ePub files available? You can upgrade to the eBook version at www.PacktPub.com and as a print book customer, you are entitled to a discount on the eBook copy. Get in touch with us at service@packtpub.com for more details.

At www.PacktPub.com, you can also read a collection of free technical articles, sign up for a range of free newsletters and receive exclusive discounts and offers on Packt books and eBooks.

https://www2.packtpub.com/books/subscription/packtlib

Do you need instant solutions to your IT questions? PacktLib is Packt's online digital book library. Here, you can search, access, and read Packt's entire library of books.

Why subscribe?

- Fully searchable across every book published by Packt
- Copy and paste, print, and bookmark content
- On demand and accessible via a web browser

Free access for Packt account holders

If you have an account with Packt at www.PacktPub.com, you can use this to access PacktLib today and view 9 entirely free books. Simply use your login credentials for immediate access.

Table of Contents

Preface

As OpenStack is now being considered to be more of a mainstream cloud platform, the challenge of operating it after it is built has become prevalent. While all cloud tasks can be executed via the API or CLI tool on a one-by-one basis, it will not be the best method to handle larger cloud deployments. The need for a more automated approach to administer OpenStack is now clear. Most organizations are seeking methods to improve business agility and have realized that just having a cloud is not enough. Being able to improve application deployments, reduce infrastructure downtime, and eliminate daily manual tasks, can only be accomplished through some sort of automation. OpenStack and Ansible will help any organization close that gap. With the IaaS capabilities that OpenStack has to offer coupled with Ansible, an easy to use configuration management tool assures a more complete cloud implementation.

Whether you are new to OpenStack or a seasoned cloud administrator, this book will aid you in managing your OpenStack cloud once it is all set up. Packed with real world OpenStack administrative tasks, we will first have a look at the working examples natively and then transition to walking through instructions on how to automate these tasks using one of the most popular open source automation tools, Ansible.

Ansible has become a market leader in the open source orchestration and automation space. With it being built using Python, similar to OpenStack, it makes for an easy marriage. The ability to leverage existing and/or new OpenStack modules will allow you to quickly move along your playbook creation.

We will start with a brief overview of OpenStack and Ansible, highlighting some of the best practices. Next, the beginning of each of the following chapters will allow you to become more familiar with handling cloud operator administration tasks, such as creating multiple users/tenants, setting up multi-tenant isolation, customizing your cloud's quotas, taking instance snapshots, deploying additional OpenStack features, running cloud health checks, and so on. Finally, each chapter will conclude with a step-by-step tutorial on how to automate these tasks with Ansible. As an added bonus, the fully functional Ansible code will be published on GitHub for your reference while reviewing the chapter and/or for later review.

Consider this book to be a 2-for-1 learning experience, a deep OpenStack-based cloud administrative knowledge and familiarity with how Ansible works. As a reader, you will be encouraged to put hands to the keyboard and give the tasks a try.

What this book covers

Chapter 1, *An Introduction to OpenStack*, is a high-level overview of OpenStack and the projects that make up this cloud platform. This introduction will set the level of the reader on the OpenStack components, concepts, and verbiage.

Chapter 2, *An Introduction to Ansible*, is a detailed review of Ansible, its features, and the best practices to use, in order to set a solid starting foundation. It reviews why leveraging Ansible to automate OpenStack tasks is the easiest option.

Chapter 3, *Creating Multiple Users/Tenants*, guides the reader through the process of creating users and tenants within OpenStack manually and the creation considerations in order to automating such a process using Ansible.

Chapter 4, *Customizing Your Cloud's Quotas*, makes you understand what quotas are and how they are used to restrict your cloud's resources. It shows the reader how to create quotas manually in OpenStack. After that, it walks the reader through how to automate this process with Ansible to take into account when handle tasks for multiple tenants at the same time.

Chapter 5, *Snapshot Your Cloud*, shows you how to create snapshots of your cloud instances manually within OpenStack and how to automate this process using Ansible. It also lets you explore the power of being able to snapshot all instances within a tenant in one shot.

Chapter 6, *Migrating Instances*, introduces the concept of migrating select instances across compute nodes in the traditional OpenStack method. It then demonstrates the required steps to automate this task while grouping instances together. It also shows the additional options that Ansible can offer in handling a task of this matter.

Chapter 7, Setting up Isolated Tenants, walks the reader through the concept of multi-tenant isolation functionality within OpenStack. It tells us about the building blocks of accomplishing this successfully and next demonstrate how to automate all the steps required to set it up. It emphasizes how automation of this level prevents incorrect configurations, missed steps, and provides an easily repeatable process.

Chapter 8, Deploying OpenStack Features, presents the process to add additional OpenStack features to your cloud with Ansible. We will use the example of multi-hypervisor support built into OpenStack, as an example to demonstrate how Ansible code can be created to deploy new features.

Chapter 9, Inventory Your Cloud, explores how the reader can dynamically inventory all the OpenStack cloud user resources with one Ansible playbook. It walks them through the necessary metrics to gather information and how that can be stored for later reference. This is a very powerful tool to have as a cloud administrator/operator.

Chapter 10, Health Check Your Cloud, demonstrates some useful tips and tricks on how to check the health of your cloud manually and leveraging Ansible to trigger hourly and/or daily reports.

What you need for this book

In order to truly benefit from this book, it is best to have deployed or have access to an OSA (OpenStack-Ansible) cloud running with the Juno release or better. The OSA deployment method provides an environment that will install both OpenStack and Ansible.

If you plan to deploy any of the other OpenStack distributions, you will still need to be running the OpenStack Juno release or better. You should also have Ansible version 1.6 or better installed on the same nodes or on your workstation.

Also, having a good text editor, such as TextWrangler, Notepad++, or Vim, will be very useful if you plan to add to or edit any of the Ansible playbooks/roles found in the GitHub repository.

Who this book is for

If you are an OpenStack-based cloud operator and/or infrastructure administrator with basic OpenStack knowledge already and are interested in automating administrative functions, then this book is exactly what you are looking for. You will take your basic OpenStack knowledge to the next level by learning how to automate simple and advanced OpenStack administration tasks. Having a functioning OpenStack environment is helpful but most certainly not required.

Conventions

In this book, you will find a number of text styles that distinguish between different kinds of information. Here are some examples of these styles and an explanation of their meaning.

Code words in text, database table names, folder names, filenames, file extensions, pathnames, dummy URLs, user input, and Twitter handles are shown as follows: "This action is accomplished by first sourcing your OpenRC file and then by executing the service-list command."

A block of code is set as follows:

```
{
"endpoints": [
{
"adminurl": "http://172.29.236.7:8774/v2/%(tenant_id)s",
"enabled": true,
"id": "90603842a5a54958a7768dd909d43237",
"internalurl": "http://172.29.236.7:8774/v2/%(tenant_id)s",
"publicurl": "http://172.29.236.7:8774/v2/%(tenant_id)s",
"region": "RegionOne",
"service_id": "020cc772b9c942eb979fc587877a9239"
},
...
```

Any command-line input or output is written as follows:

```
$ keystone endpoint-list
```

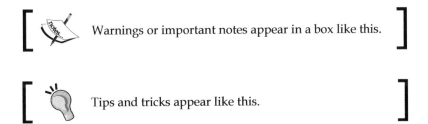

Warnings or important notes appear in a box like this.

Tips and tricks appear like this.

Reader feedback

Feedback from our readers is always welcome. Let us know what you think about this book—what you liked or disliked. Reader feedback is important for us as it helps us develop titles that you will really get the most out of.

To send us general feedback, simply e-mail feedback@packtpub.com, and mention the book's title in the subject of your message.

If there is a topic that you have expertise in and you are interested in either writing or contributing to a book, see our author guide at www.packtpub.com/authors.

Customer support

Now that you are the proud owner of a Packt book, we have a number of things to help you to get the most from your purchase.

Downloading the example code

You can download the example code files from your account at http://www.packtpub.com for all the Packt Publishing books you have purchased. If you purchased this book elsewhere, you can visit http://www.packtpub.com/support and register to have the files e-mailed directly to you.

Errata

Although we have taken every care to ensure the accuracy of our content, mistakes do happen. If you find a mistake in one of our books—maybe a mistake in the text or the code—we would be grateful if you could report this to us. By doing so, you can save other readers from frustration and help us improve subsequent versions of this book. If you find any errata, please report them by visiting http://www.packtpub.com/submit-errata, selecting your book, clicking on the **Errata Submission Form** link, and entering the details of your errata. Once your errata are verified, your submission will be accepted and the errata will be uploaded to our website or added to any list of existing errata under the Errata section of that title.

To view the previously submitted errata, go to https://www.packtpub.com/books/content/support and enter the name of the book in the search field. The required information will appear under the **Errata** section.

Piracy

Piracy of copyrighted material on the Internet is an ongoing problem across all media. At Packt, we take the protection of our copyright and licenses very seriously. If you come across any illegal copies of our works in any form on the Internet, please provide us with the location address or website name immediately so that we can pursue a remedy.

Please contact us at copyright@packtpub.com with a link to the suspected pirated material.

We appreciate your help in protecting our authors and our ability to bring you valuable content.

Questions

If you have a problem with any aspect of this book, you can contact us at questions@packtpub.com, and we will do our best to address the problem.

1
An Introduction to OpenStack

This chapter will serve as an overview of OpenStack and all the projects that make up this cloud platform. It is very important to lay a clear foundation of OpenStack, in order to describe the OpenStack components, concepts, and verbiage. Once the overview is covered, we will transition into discussing the core features and benefits of OpenStack. Lastly, the chapter will finish up with two working examples of how you can consume the OpenStack services via the **application program interface (API)** and **command-line interface (CLI)**. In this chapter, we will cover the following points:

- OpenStack overview
- Reviewing the OpenStack services
- OpenStack supporting components
- The features and benefits
- Working examples: listing the services and endpoints

OpenStack overview

In the simplest definition possible, OpenStack can be described as an open source cloud operating platform that can be used to control large pools of compute, storage, and networking resources throughout a data center. It is all managed through a single interface controlled by either an API, CLI, and/or web **graphical user interface (GUI)** dashboard. The power that OpenStack offers the administrators is the ability to control all these resources, while still empowering the cloud consumers to provision the same resources through other self-service models. OpenStack was built in a modular fashion; the platform is made up of numerous components. Some of the components are considered as core services and are required in order to have a functional cloud, while the other services are optional and are only required unless they fit into your personal use case.

The OpenStack foundation

Back in early 2010 Rackspace, at that time was just a technology hosting company focused on providing service and support thru an offering called "Fanatical Support", decided to create an open source cloud platform. After two years of managing the OpenStack project with its 25 initial partners, it was decided to transfer the intellectual property and governance of OpenStack to a non-profit member run foundation that is known as the OpenStack Foundation.

The OpenStack Foundation is made up of voluntary members governed by an appointed board of directors and project based tech committees. The collaboration occurs around a six-month, time-based major code release cycle. The release names are run in alphabetical order and refer to the region encompassing the location where the OpenStack design summit will be held. Each release incorporates something called OpenStack Design Summit, which is meant to build collaboration among OpenStack operators/consumers; thus, allowing the project developers to have live working sessions and also agree on release items.

As an OpenStack Foundation member, you can take an active role in helping develop any of the OpenStack projects. There is no other cloud platform that allows such participation.

To learn more about the OpenStack Foundation, you can go to the `www.openstack.org` website.

Reviewing the OpenStack services

Getting to the heart of what makes up OpenStack as a project would be to review the services that make up this cloud ecosystem. One thing to be kept in mind in reference to the OpenStack services is that each service will have an official name and a code name associated with it. The use of the code name has become very popular among the community and most documentation will refer to the services in that manner. Thus, becoming familiar with the code names is important and will ease the adoption process.

The other thing to be kept in mind is that each service is developed as an API driven REST web service. All the actions are executed via the API, enabling ultimate consumption flexibility. Behind the scenes, API calls are executed and interpreted even while using the CLI or web-based GUI.

As of the Kilo release, the OpenStack project consists of twelve services/programs. The services will be reviewed in the order of their release to show an overall service timeline. That timeline will show the natural progression of the OpenStack project overall, also showing how it is now surely Enterprise ready.

OpenStack Compute (codename Nova)

It was integrated in the release *Austin* and was one of the first and is still the most important service part of the OpenStack platform. Nova is the component that provides the bridge to the underlying hypervisor, which is used to manage the computing resources.

 One common misunderstanding is that Nova is a hypervisor in itself, which is simply not true. Nova is a hypervisor manager of sorts and is capable of supporting many different types of hypervisors.

Nova will be responsible for scheduling instance creation, sizing options for the instance, managing the instance location, and, as mentioned earlier, keeping track of the hypervisors available to the cloud environment. It also handles the functionality of segregating your cloud into isolation groups called cells, regions, and availability zones.

OpenStack Object Storage (codename Swift)

It was also integrated in the *Austin* release and this service is one of the first services that were a part of the OpenStack platform. Swift is the component that provides *object storage* as a *service* to your OpenStack cloud. It is capable of storing petabytes of data; in turn, adding highly available, distributed, and eventually consistent object/blob store. Object storage is intended to be a cheap and cost effective storage solution for static data such as images, backups, archives, and static content. The objects can then be streamed over standard web protocols (HTTP/HTTPS), to or from the object server to the end user initiating the web request. The other key feature of Swift is that all data is automatically made available as it is replicated across the cluster. The storage cluster is meant to scale horizontally, by simply adding new servers.

OpenStack Image Service (codename Glance)

It was integrated in the *Bextar* release and this service was introduced during the second OpenStack release and is responsible for managing/registering/maintaining server images for your OpenStack cloud. It includes the capability to upload or export OpenStack compatible images and store instance snapshots, and is used as a template/backup for later use. Glance can store the images on a variety of locations either locally and/or on distributed storage, such as object storage. Most Linux kernel distributions already have OpenStack compatible images available for download. You can also create your own server images from existing servers. There exists support for multiple image formats including: RAW, VHD, QCOW2, VMDK, OVF, and VDI.

OpenStack Identity (codename Keystone)

It was integrated in the *Essex* release and this service was introduced during the fifth OpenStack release. Keystone is the authentication and authorization component built into your OpenStack cloud. Its key role is to handle creation, registry, and management of users, tenants, and all the other OpenStack services. Keystone is the first component to be installed when starting an OpenStack cloud. It has the capability to connect to external directory services, such as LDAP. Another key feature of Keystone is that it is built based on **role-based access controls (RBAC)**, thus allowing cloud operators to provide distinct role-based access to individual service features to the cloud consumers.

OpenStack Dashboard (codename Horizon)

It was also integrated in the *Essex* release and this service is the second service to be introduced in the fifth OpenStack release. Horizon provides cloud operators and consumers with a web based GUI to control their compute, storage, and network resources. The OpenStack dashboard runs on top of Apache and the Django REST framework; thus, making it very easy to integrate into and extend to meet your personal use case. On the backend, Horizon also uses the native OpenStack APIs. The basic principle behind Horizon was to be able to provide cloud operators with a quick and overall view of the state of their cloud and cloud consumers a self-service provisioning portal to the cloud resources designated to them.

Note that horizon can handle approximately 70% of the overall available OpenStack functionality. To leverage 100% of the OpenStack functionality, you will need to utilize the API's directly and/or utilize the CLI for each service.

OpenStack Networking (codename Neutron)

It was integrated in the *Folsom* release and this service is probably the second most powerful component within your OpenStack cloud next to Nova.

OpenStack Networking is intended to provide a pluggable, scalable, and API-driven system to manage networks and IP addresses.

This quote was taken directly from the OpenStack Networking documentation, as it best reflects exactly the purpose behind Neutron. Neutron is responsible to create your virtual networks with your OpenStack cloud. This will entail the creation of virtual networks, routers, subnets, firewalls, load balancers, and similar network functions. Neutron was developed with an extension framework, which allows the integration of additional network components (physical network device control) and models (flat, layer-2 and/or layer-3 networks). The various vendor specific plugins and adapters have been created to work in line with Neutron. This service adds to the self-service aspect of OpenStack; thus, removing the network aspect from being a roadblock to consume your cloud.

With Neutron being one of the most advanced and powerful components within OpenStack, a whole book was dedicated to it.

OpenStack Block Storage (codename Cinder)

It was also integrated in the *Folsom* release, Cinder is the component that provides block storage as a service to your OpenStack cloud by leveraging local disks or attached storage devices. This translates into persistent block level storage volumes available to your instances. Cinder is responsible for managing and maintaining the block volumes created, attaching/detaching those volumes, and also backup creation of that volume. One of the highly notable features of Cinder is its ability to connect to multiple types of backend shared storage platforms at the same time. This capability spectrum spans all the way down to being able to leverage simple Linux server storage as well. As an added bonus, **Quality of Service (QoS)** roles can be applied to different types of backends; thus, extending the ability to use the block storage devices to meet various application requirements.

OpenStack Orchestration (codename Heat)

It was integrated in the *Havana* release and this was one of the two services to be introduced in the eighth OpenStack release. Heat provides the orchestration capability over your OpenStack cloud resource. It is described as a main-line project part of the OpenStack orchestration program. This infers the additional automation functionality that is in the pipeline for OpenStack.

The built-in orchestration engine is used to automate provisioning of applications and its components, known as stack. A stack might include instances, networks, subnets, routers, ports, router interfaces, security groups, security group rules, auto scaling rules, and so on. Heat utilizes templates to define a stack and is written in a standard markup format, YAML. You will notice these templates being referred to as **Heat Orchestration Template (HOT)** templates.

OpenStack Telemetry (codename Ceilometer)

It was also integrated in the *Havana* release and this is the second of the two services introduced in the eighth OpenStack release. Ceilometer collects the cloud usage and performance statistics together into one centralized data store. This capability becomes a key component to a cloud operator as it gives clear metrics into the overall cloud, which can be used to make scaling decisions.

 You have the option of choosing the data store backend to Ceilometer. Such options include: MongoDB, MySQL, PostgreSQL, HBase, and DB2.

OpenStack Database (codename Trove)

It was integrated in the *Icehouse* release, Trove is the component that provides database as a service to your OpenStack cloud. This capability includes providing scalable and reliable relational and non-relational database engines. The goal behind this service was to remove the burden of needing to understand database installation and administration. With Trove, the cloud consumers can provision database instances just by leveraging the services API. Trove supports multiple single-tenant databases within a Nova instance.

 The following data store types are currently supported by OpenStack: MySQL, MongoDB, Cassandra, Redis and CouchDB.

OpenStack Data Processing (codename Sahara)

It was integrated in the *Juno* release, Sahara is the component that provides data processing as a service to your OpenStack cloud. This capability includes the ability to provision an application cluster tuned to handle large amounts of analytical data. The data store options available are Hadoop and/or Spark. This service will also aid the cloud consumer in being able to abstract the complication of installing and maintaining this type of cluster.

OpenStack Bare Metal Provisioning (codename Ironic)

It was integrated in the *Kilo* release and this service has been one of the most anxiously awaited components of the OpenStack project. Ironic provides the capability to provision physical bare metal servers from within your OpenStack cloud. It is commonly known as a bare metal hypervisor API and leverages a set of plugins to enable interaction with the bare metal servers. It is the newest service to be introduced to the OpenStack family and is still under development.

OpenStack supporting components

It is similar to any traditional application, there are dependent core components that are pivotal to the functionality but not necessarily the application itself. In the case of the base OpenStack architecture, there are two core components that will be considered as the core or backbone of the cloud. The OpenStack functionality requires access to an SQL-based backend database service and an **Advanced Message Queuing Protocol (AMQP)** software platform. Just as with most things OpenStack related there are the most commonly used/recommended choices adopted by the OpenStack community. From a database perspective, the common choice will be MySQL and the default AMQP package is RabbitMQ. These two dependencies must be installed, configured, and functional before you can start an OpenStack deployment.

There are additional optional software packages that can also be used to provide further stability as a part of your cloud design. The information about this management software and OpenStack architecture details can be found at the following link:

http://docs.openstack.org/arch-design/generalpurpose-architecture.html

Features and benefits

The power of OpenStack has been tested true by numerous Enterprise grade organizations; thus, gaining the focus of many of the leading IT companies. As this adoption increases, we will surely see an increase in consumption and additional improved features/functionality. For now, let's review some of OpenStack's features and benefits.

Fully distributed architecture

Every service within the OpenStack platform can be grouped together and/or separated to meet your personal use case. Also, as mentioned earlier, only the core services (Keystone, Nova, and Glance) are required to have a functioning cloud; all other components can be optional. This level of flexibility is something every administrator seeks for an **Infrastructure as a Service (IaaS)** platform.

Uses commodity hardware

OpenStack was uniquely designed to accommodate almost any type of hardware. The underlying OS is the only dependency of OpenStack. As long as OpenStack supports the underlying OS and that OS is supported on the particular hardware, you are all set to go! There is no requirement to purchase OEM hardware or even hardware with specific specs. This gives yet another level of deployment flexibility for administrators. Good example of this can be giving your old hardware sitting around in your data center new life within an OpenStack cloud.

Scale horizontally or vertically

The ability to easily scale your cloud is another key feature to OpenStack. Adding additional compute nodes is as simple as installing the necessary OpenStack services on the new server. The same process is used to expand the OpenStack services control plane as well. Just as with other platforms, you can add more computing resources to any node as an alternate approach to scaling up.

Meets high availability requirements

OpenStack is able to certify meeting high availability (99.9%) requirements for its own infrastructure services, if implemented via the documented best practices.

Compute isolation and multi-DC support

Another key feature of OpenStack is the support to handle compute hypervisor isolation and the ability to support multiple OpenStack regions across data centers. Compute isolation includes the ability to separate multiple pools of hypervisors distinguished by hypervisor type, hardware similarity, and/or vCPU ratio.

The ability to support multiple OpenStack regions, which is a complete installation of functioning OpenStack clouds with shared services, such as Keystone and Horizon, across data centers is a key function to maintain highly available infrastructure. This model eases overall cloud administration; thus, allowing a single pane of glass to manage multiple clouds.

Robust role-based access control

All the OpenStack services allow RBAC while assigning authorization to cloud consumers. This gives cloud operators the ability to decide the specific functions allowed by the cloud consumers. An appropriate example will be to grant a cloud user the ability to create instances but denying the ability to upload new server images or adjust instance-sizing options.

Working examples – list the services and endpoints

So we have covered what OpenStack is, the services that make up OpenStack, and some of the key features of OpenStack. It is only appropriate to show a working example of the OpenStack functionality and the methods available to manage/administer your OpenStack cloud.

To re-emphasize, OpenStack management, administration, and consumption of services can be accomplished either by an API, CLI, and/or web dashboard. When considering some level of automation, the last option of the web dashboard is normally not involved. So, for the remainder of this book, we will solely focus on using the OpenStack APIs and CLIs.

Listing the OpenStack services

Now, let's take a look at how you can use either the OpenStack API or CLI to check for the available services and endpoints active within your cloud. We will first start with listing the available services.

Via API

The first step in using the OpenStack services is authentication against Keystone. You must always first authenticate (tell the API who you are) and then receive authorization (API ingests your username and determines what predefined task(s) you can execute) based on what your user is allowed to do. That complete process ends with providing you with an authentication token.

The Keystone can provide two different types of token formats: UUID or PKI. A typical UUID token looks similar to `53f7f6ef0cc344b5be706bcc8b1479e1`. While a PKI token is a much longer string and harder to work with. It is suggested to set Keystone to provide UUID tokens within your cloud.

In the following section, there is an example of making an authentication request for a secure token. Making API requests using **cURL**, a useful tool to interact with RESTful APIs, is the easiest approach. Using cURL with various options, you can simulate actions similar to ones using the OpenStack CLI or the Horizon dashboard:

```
$ curl -d @credentials.json -X POST -H "Content-Type: application/json"
http://127.0.0.1:5000/v2.0/tokens | python -mjson.tool
```

> Since the credential string is fairly long and easy to manipulate incorrectly, it is suggested to utilize the -d @<filename> functionality part of cURL. This allows you to insert the credential string into a file and then pass it into your API request by just referencing the file. This exercise is very similar to creating a client environment script (also known as OpenRC files).
>
> Adding | python -mjson.tool to the end of your API request makes the JSON output easier to read.

The following is an example of the credential string:

```
{"auth": {"tenantName": "admin", "passwordCredentials": {"username":
"raxuser", "password": "raxpasswd"}}}
```

When the example is executed against the Keystone API, it will respond with an authentication token. That token should be used for all subsequent API requests. Keep in mind that the token does expire, but traditionally, a token is configured to last 24 hours from the creation timestamp.

The `token` can be found in the second to last section of the JSON output, in the section labeled `token` as shown in the following code snippet:

```
"token": {
"audit_ids": [
"tWnOdGc-Qpu71Ag6QUo9JQ"
],
"expires": "2015-06-30T04:53:27Z",
"id": "907ca229af164a09918a661ffa224747",
"issued_at": "2015-06-29T16:53:27.191192",
"tenant": {
"description": "Admin Tenant",
"enabled": true,
"id": "4cc43830491046ada1f0f26317da41c0",
"name": "admin"
}
}
```

Once you have the authentication token, you can begin crafting subsequent API requests to request information about your cloud and/or execute tasks. Now, we will request the list of services available in your cloud, using the following command:

```
$ curl -X GET http://127.0.0.1:35357/v2.0/OS-KSADM/services -H "Accept:
application/json" -H "X-Auth-Token: 907ca229af164a09918a661ffa224747" |
python -mjson.tool
```

The output from this API request will be the complete list of services registered within your cloud by name, description, type, id, and whether it is active. An abstract of the output will look similar to the following code block:

```
{
"OS-KSADM:services": [
{
"description": "Nova Compute Service",
"enabled": true,
"id": "020cc772b9c942eb979fc587877a9239",
"name": "nova",
"type": "compute"
},
{
"description": "Nova Compute Service V3",
"enabled": true,
"id": "1565c929d84b423fb3c9561b22e4468c",
"name": "novav3",
"type": "computev3"
},
...
```

Via CLI

All the base principles applied to using the API in the preceding section also applies to using the CLI. The major difference with the CLI is that all you need to do is create an OpenRC file with your credentials and execute defined commands. The CLI handles the formatting of the API calls behind the scenes and also takes care of grabbing the token for subsequent requests and even handles formatting the output.

As discussed earlier, first you need to authenticate against Keystone to be granted a secure token. This action is accomplished by first sourcing your OpenRC file and then by executing the service-list command. The following example will demonstrate this in more detail.

Here is an example of an OpenRC file named `openrc`:

```
# To use an OpenStack cloud you need to authenticate against keystone.
export OS_ENDPOINT_TYPE=internalURL
export OS_USERNAME=admin
export OS_TENANT_NAME=admin
export OS_AUTH_URL=http://127.0.0.1:5000/v2.0

# With Keystone you pass the keystone password.
echo "Please enter your OpenStack Password: "
read -sr OS_PASSWORD_INPUT
export OS_PASSWORD=$OS_PASSWORD_INPUT
```

Once you create and source the OpenRC file, you can begin using the CLI to execute commands, such as requesting the list of services; you can follow the following working example:

```
$ source openrc
$ keystone service-list
```

The output will look similar to this:

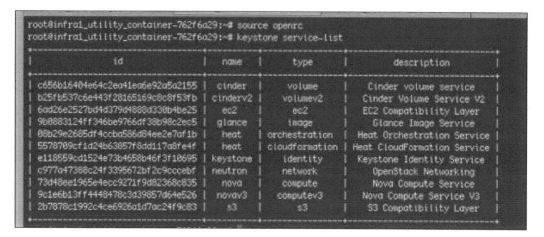

Listing the OpenStack endpoints

We will now move onto listing the available endpoints registered within your cloud. You will note that the process is very similar to the previous steps just explained.

Via API

Since we are already authenticated against Keystone in the previous example, we can just execute the following command to get back the full list of API endpoints available for your OpenStack cloud.

```
$ curl -X GET http://127.0.0.1:35357/v2.0/endpoints -H "Accept:
application/json" -H "X-Auth-Token: 907ca229af164a09918a661ffa224747" |
python -mjson.tool
```

The output of this API request will be the complete list of endpoints registered within your cloud by `adminurl`, `internalurl`, `publicurl`, `region`, `service_id`, `id`, and whether it is active. An abstract of the output will look similar to the following code block:

```
{
"endpoints": [
{
"adminurl": "http://172.29.236.7:8774/v2/%(tenant_id)s",
"enabled": true,
"id": "90603842a5a54958a7768dd909d43237",
"internalurl": "http://172.29.236.7:8774/v2/%(tenant_id)s",
"publicurl": "http://172.29.236.7:8774/v2/%(tenant_id)s",
"region": "RegionOne",
"service_id": "020cc772b9c942eb979fc587877a9239"
},
...
```

Via CLI

As with the earlier CLI request, after sourcing the OpenRC file you will simply execute the following command:

```
$ keystone endpoint-list
```

The output will look similar to the following screenshot:

Downloading the example code

You can download the example code files from your account at http://www.packtpub.com for all the Packt Publishing books you have purchased. If you purchased this book elsewhere, you can visit http://www.packtpub.com/support and register to have the files e-mailed directly to you.

Summary

At this point in the book, you should have a clear understanding of OpenStack and how to use the various services that make up your OpenStack cloud. Also, you should be able to communicate some of the key features and benefits to using OpenStack.

We will now transition into learning about Ansible and why using it in conjunction with OpenStack is a great combination.

2
An Introduction to Ansible

This chapter will serve as a high-level overview of Ansible and the components that make up this open source configuration management tool. We will cover defining the Ansible components and their typical use, break down how to define variables for the roles, and defining and setting facts about the hosts for the playbooks. Next, we will transition into the ways with which you can define the host inventory used to run your playbooks against. Lastly, the chapter will wind up with a working example of a playbook that will confirm the required host connectivity needed to utilize Ansible. In this chapter, we will cover the following topics:

- Ansible overview
- What are playbooks, roles, and modules?
- Variables and facts
- Defining the inventory

Ansible overview

Ansible in its simplest form has been described as a Python-based open source IT automation tool that can be used to configure\manage systems, deploy software (or almost anything), and provide orchestration to a process. These are just a few of the many possible use cases for Ansible. In my previous life, as a production support infrastructure engineer, I wish such a tool existed, so that I could have had much more sleep and a lot less grey hair.

One thing that always stood out to me in regards to Ansible is that the developer's first and foremost goal was to create a tool that offers **simplicity and maximum ease of use**. In a world filled with complicated and intricate software, keeping it simple goes a long way for most IT professionals.

Sticking to the goal of keeping things simple, Ansible handles configuration/ management of hosts solely through **Secure Shell (SSH)** and absolutely no daemon or agent is required; the server or workstation where you run the playbooks from only needs Python and a few other packages, most likely already present, installed. Honestly, it does not get simpler than this.

The automation code used with Ansible is organized into something called playbooks and roles, which is written in the YAML markup format. Ansible follows the YAML formatting and structure within the playbooks/roles. Being familiar with YAML formatting helps you while creating your playbooks/roles. If you are not familiar with it, do not worry, as it is very easy to pick up (it is all about the spaces and dashes).

The playbooks and roles are in a non-complied format and making the code is very simple to read, if you are familiar with standard Unix\Linux commands. There is also a suggested directory structure to create playbooks. One of my favorite features of Ansible is enabling the ability to review and/or utilize playbooks written by anyone else with little to no direction needed.

 I strongly suggest that you review the Ansible playbook best practices before getting started at `http://docs.ansible.com/playbooks_best_practices.html`. I also find the overall Ansible website very intuitive and filled with great examples at `http://docs.ansible.com`.

My favorite excerpt from the Ansible playbook best practices is under the *Content Organization* section. Having a clear understanding of how to organize your automation code proved very helpful to me. The following is the suggested directory layout for playbooks:

```
group_vars/
    group1              # here we assign variables to particular groups
    group2              # ""
host_vars/
    hostname1           # if systems need specific variables, put them
here
    hostname2           # ""

library/                # if any custom modules, put them here (optional)
filter_plugins/         # if any custom filter plugins, put them here
(optional)

site.yml                # master playbook
webservers.yml          # playbook for webserver tier
dbservers.yml           # playbook for dbserver tier
```

```
roles/
    tasks/              #
        main.yml        #  <-- tasks file can include smaller files
    handlers/           #
        main.yml        #  <-- handlers file
    templates/          #  <-- files for use with the template resource
        ntp.conf.j2     #  <------- templates end in .j2
    files/              #
        bar.txt         #  <-- files for use with the copy resource
        foo.sh          #  <-- script files for use with the script
    vars/               #
        main.yml        #  <-- variables associated with this role
    defaults/           #
        main.yml        #  <-- default lower priority variables for this
role
    meta/               #
        main.yml        #  <-- role dependencie
```

It is now time to dig deeper into reviewing what playbooks, roles, and modules consist of. This is where we will break down each of these components according to their distinct purposes.

What are playbooks, roles, and modules?

The automation code that you will create to be run by Ansible is broken down into hierarchical layers. Envision a pyramid with its multiple levels of elevation. We will start at the top and discuss **playbooks** first.

Playbooks

Imagine that a playbook is the very topmost triangle of a pyramid. A playbook takes on the role of executing all of the lower level codes contained in a role. It can also be seen as a wrapper to the roles created; we will cover the roles in the next section.

The playbooks also contain other high level runtime parameters, such as the host(s) to run the playbook against, the root user to use, and/or if the playbook needs to be run as a sudo user. These are just a few of the many playbook parameters you can add. The following is an example of what the syntax of a playbook looks similar to:

```
---
# Sample playbooks structure/syntax.

- hosts: dbservers
user: root
remote_user: root
```

```
sudo: yes
roles:
    - mysql-install
```

> In the preceding example, you will notice that the playbook begins with
> ---. This is required as the heading (line 1) for each playbook and role.
>
> Also, please note the spacing structure at the beginning of each line. The
> easiest way to remember it is that each main command starts with a dash
> (-). Then every sub-command starts with two spaces and repeats the
> lower you go in the code hierarchy. As we walk through more examples,
> it will start to make more sense.

Let's go through the above example and break down the sections. The first step in
the playbook was to define what hosts to run the playbook against; in this case it was
dbservers (which can be a single host or a list of hosts). The next area sets the user
to run the playbook as locally, remotely, and enable executing the playbook as sudo.
The last section of the syntax lists the roles to be executed.

The preceding example is similar to the formatting of the other playbooks, which you
will see in the next chapters. This format incorporates defining roles, which allows
scaling out playbooks and reusability (you will find most advanced playbooks
structured this way). With Ansible's high level of flexibility, you can also create
playbooks in a simpler consolidated format, as shown in the following example:

```
---
# Sample simple playbooks structure/syntax

- name: Install MySQL Playbook
hosts: dbservers
user: root
remote_user: root
sudo: yes
tasks:
    - name: Install MySQL
apt: name={{item}} state=present
with_items:
        - libselinux-python
        - mysql
        - mysql-server
        - MySQL-python
```

```
    - name: Copying my.cnf configuration file
template: src=cust_my.cnfdest=/etc/my.cnf mode=0755

    - name: Prep MySQL db
command: chdir=/usr/bin mysql_install_db

    - name: Enable MySQL to be started at boot
service: name=mysqld enabled=yes state=restarted

    - name: Prep MySQL db
command: chdir=/usr/bin mysqladmin -u root password 'passwd'
```

Now that we have reviewed what playbooks are, we will move on to reviewing roles and their benefits.

Roles

Moving down to the next level of the Ansible pyramid, we will now discuss **roles**. The most effective way to describe roles is the breaking up of a playbook into multiple smaller files. So instead of having one long playbook with multiple tasks defined, all handling separately related steps, you can now break the playbook into individual specific roles. This format keeps your playbooks simple and gives you the ability to reuse roles between playbooks.

> The best advice I personally received concerning creating roles is to keep them simple. Try to create a role to do a specific function, such as install a software package. You can then create a second role to just do configurations. In this format, you can reuse the initial installation role over and over without needing to make code changes for the next project.

The typical syntax of a role can be found in the following example and will be placed into a file named `main.yml` within the `roles/<name of role>/tasks` directory:

```
---
- name: Install MySQL
apt: name={{item}} state=present
with_items:
    - libselinux-python
    - mysql
    - mysql-server
    - MySQL-python
```

```
- name: Copying my.cnf configuration file
template: src=cust_my.cnfdest=/etc/my.cnf mode=0755

- name: Prep MySQL db
command: chdir=/usr/bin mysql_install_db

- name: Enable MySQL to be started at boot
service: name=mysqld enabled=yes state=restarted

- name: Prep MySQL db
command: chdir=/usr/bin mysqladmin -u root password 'passwd'
```

The complete structure of a role is identified in the directory layout found in the *Ansible overview* section of this chapter. In the next chapter, we will review additional functions of roles as we step through the working examples. Now that we have covered playbooks and roles we are prepared to move over to the last topic in this session, which is modules.

Modules

Another key feature of Ansible is that it comes with a predefined code that can control system functions, called **modules**. The modules are executed directly against the remote host(s) or via playbooks. The execution of a module generally requires you to pass a set number of arguments. The Ansible website (`http://docs.ansible.com/modules_by_category.html`) does a great job of documenting every available module and the possible arguments to pass to that module.

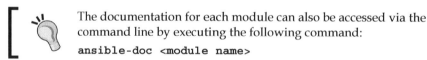

> The documentation for each module can also be accessed via the command line by executing the following command:
>
> `ansible-doc <module name>`

The use of modules will always be the recommended approach within Ansible, as they are written to avoid making the requested change to the host unless the change needs to be made. This is very useful when re-executing a playbook against a host more than once. The modules are smart enough to know that the steps that have already completed successfully do not need to be re-executed, unless some argument or command is changed.

Referring to the role example shared earlier, you will note the use of various modules. The modules used are highlighted again in the following example to provide further clarity:

```
---
- name: Install MySQL
  apt: name={{item}} state=present
  with_items:
      - libselinux-python
      - mysql
      - mysql-server
      - MySQL-python

- name: Copying my.cnf configuration file
  template: src=cust_my.cnfdest=/etc/my.cnf mode=0755

- name: Prep MySQL db
  command: chdir=/usr/bin mysql_install_db

- name: Enable MySQL to be started at boot
  service: name=mysqld enabled=yes state=restarted
...
```

Another feature worth mentioning is that not only can you utilize the current modules, you can also write your very own modules. While the core of Ansible is written in Python, your modules can be written in almost any language. Underneath it, all the modules technically return JSON format data, thus enabling language flexibility.

In this section, we were able to cover the top two sections of our Ansible pyramid, playbooks, and roles. We also reviewed the use of modules—the built-in power behind Ansible. Now, we will transition into another key feature of Ansible: variable substitution and gathering host facts.

Variables and facts

Anyone who has ever attempted to create some sort of automation code, whether via Bash or Perl scripts, knows that being able to define variables is an essential component. While Ansible does not compare to other programming languages mentioned, it does contain some core programming language features, such as variable substitution.

Variables

To start, let's first define the meaning of variables and use it in the event that this is a new concept. Wikipedia defines it as:

> *Variable (computer science), a symbolic name associated with a value and whose associated value may be changed.*

Using a variable allows you to set a symbolic placeholder in your automation code that you can substitute values for, on each execution. Ansible accommodates defining variables within your playbooks and roles in various ways. When dealing with OpenStack and/or cloud technologies in general, being able to adjust your execution parameters on the fly is critical.

We will see a few ways in which you can set variable placeholders in your playbooks, how to define variable values, and how you can register the result of a task as a variable.

Setting variable placeholders

In the event you want to set a variable placeholder within your playbooks, you will add the following syntax, as shown:

```
- name: Copying my.cnf configuration file
  template: src=cust_my.cnfdest={{ CONFIG_LOC }} mode=0755
```

In the above example, the variable CONFIG_LOC was added in place of the configuration file location (/etc/my.cnf) designated in the earlier example. When setting the placeholder, the variable name must be encased within {{ }}, as shown in the example.

Defining variable values

Now that you have added the variable to your playbook, you must define the variable value. This can be done easily by passing command-line values, such as the following:

```
$ ansible-playbook base.yml --extra-vars "CONFIG_LOC=/etc/my.cnf"
```

Or you can define the values directly in your playbook, within each role, or include them inside of global playbook variable files. The following are examples of the three options.

Define the variable value directly in your playbook by adding the `vars` section:

```
---
# Sample simple playbooks structure/syntax

- name: Install MySQL Playbook
hosts: dbservers
...
vars:
    CONFIG_LOC: /etc/my.cnf
...
```

Define the variable value within each role by creating a variable file named `main.yml` within the `vars/` directory of the role with the following contents:

```
---
CONFIG_LOC: /etc/my.cnf
```

To define a variable value inside of the global playbook, you first need to create a host specific to a variable file within the `group_vars/` directory in the root of the playbook directory with the exact same contents as discussed earlier. In this case, the variable file must be named to match the host or host group name defined within the `hosts` file.

As shown in the preceding example, the host group name is `dbservers`, in turn a file named `dbservers` will be created within the `group_vars/` directory.

Registering variables

A situation at times arises when you want to capture the output of a task. Within the process of capturing the result, you are in essence registering a dynamic variable. This type of variable is slightly different from the standard variables that we have covered so far.

Here is an example of registering the result of a task to a variable:

```
- name: Check Keystone process
  shell: ps -ef | grep keystone
  register: keystone_check
```

The registered variable value data structure can be stored in a few formats. It will always follow a base JSON format, but the value can be stored under different attributes. Personally, I have found it difficult at times to blindly determine the format and that is why the following tip will save you hours of troubleshooting.

To review and have the data structure of a registered variable returned when running a playbook, you can use the debug module, such as adding - debug: var=keystone_check to the previous example.

Facts

When Ansible runs a playbook, one of the first things it does on your behalf is gather facts about the host before executing tasks or roles. The information gathered about the host will range from the base information, such as operating system and IP addresses or going into detailed information, such as the hardware type/resources. The details captured are then stored into a variable called **facts**.

You can find a complete list of available facts on the Ansible website:

```
http://docs.ansible.com/playbooks_variables.html#information-
discovered-from-systems-facts
```

 You have the option to disable the facts gathering process by adding the gather_facts: false to your playbook. Facts about a host are captured by default, unless the feature is disabled.

A quick way of viewing all the facts associated with a host is to manually execute the following code via the command line:

```
$ ansible dbservers -m setup
```

There is plenty more you can do with facts and I will encourage you to take some time to review them in the Ansible documentation. Next, we will learn more about the base of our pyramid, the host inventory. Without an inventory of hosts to run, the playbooks against you will be creating the automation code for nothing.

So, to end this chapter we will dig deeper into how Ansible handles host inventory, whether it be in a static and/or dynamic format.

Defining the inventory

The process of defining a collection of hosts to Ansible is called the **inventory**. A host can be defined using its **Fully Qualified Domain Name (FQDN)**, local hostname, and/or its IP address. Since Ansible uses SSH to connect to the hosts, you can provide any alias for the host that the machine where Ansible is installed can understand.

Ansible expects the *inventory file* to be in an INI-like format and named **hosts**. By default, the inventory file is usually located in the `/etc/ansible` directory and will look something similar to this:

```
athena.example.com

[ocean]
aegaeon.example.com
ceto.example.com

[air]
aeolus.example.com
zeus.example.com
apollo.example.com
```

> Personally, I have found the default inventory file to be located in different places depending on the operating system Ansible is installed on. With that point, I prefer to use the `-i` command line option when executing a playbook. This allows me to designate the specific `hosts` file location. A working example will look similar to this: `ansible-playbook -i hosts base.yml`.

In the preceding example, there is a single host and a group of hosts defined. The hosts are grouped together into a group by defining a group name enclosed in `[ ]` inside the inventory file. Two groups are defined in the above example: *ocean* and *air*.

In the event where you do not have any hosts within your inventory file, (such as in the case of running a playbook locally only) you can add the following entry to define a localhost, such as this:

```
[localhost]
localhostansible_connection=local
```

The option exists to define a variable for hosts and a group inside of your inventory file. More of the information on how to do this and additional inventory details can be found on the Ansible website at `http://docs.ansible.com/intro_inventory.html`.

Dynamic inventory

It seemed appropriate since we are automating functions on a cloud platform to review yet another great feature of Ansible, which is the ability to dynamically capture an inventory of hosts/instances. One of the primary principles of cloud is to be able to create instances on-demand directly via an API, GUI, CLI, and/or through automation code, such as Ansible. That basic principle will make relying on a static inventory file pretty much a useless choice. This is why you will need to rely heavily on **dynamic inventory**.

A dynamic inventory script can be created to pull information from your cloud at runtime and then in turn use that information for the playbook's execution. Ansible provides the functionality to detect if an inventory file is set as an executable and if so, will it execute the script to pull current time inventory data.

 Since creating an Ansible dynamic inventory script is considered more of an advanced activity, I am going to direct you to the Ansible website, as they have a few working examples of dynamic inventory scripts there (http://docs.ansible.com/intro_dynamic_inventory.html).

Fortunately, in our case we will be reviewing an OpenStack cloud built using **OpenStack Ansible Deployment (OSAD)**. OSAD comes with a pre-built dynamic inventory script that will work for your OpenStack cloud. The script is named dynamic_inventory.py and can be found within the playbooks/inventory directory located in the root OSAD deployment folder. In the next chapters, you will see the working example of how to leverage this dynamic inventory file. A simple example of how to use the dynamic inventory file can be seen in the next example.

First, execute the dynamic inventory script manually to become familiar with the data structure and group names defined (this example assumes that you are in the root OSAD deployment directory):

```
$ cd playbooks/inventory
$ ./dynamic_inventory.py
```

This will print to the screen an output similar to the following:

```
    ...
    },
        "compute_all": {
            "hosts": [
                "compute1_rsyslog_container-19482f86",
                "compute1",
```

```
                "compute2_rsyslog_container-dee00ea5",
                "compute2"
        ]
    },
    "utility_container": {
        "hosts": [
            "infra1_utility_container-c5589031"
        ]
    },
    "nova_spice_console": {
        "hosts": [
            "infra1_nova_spice_console_container-dd12200f"
        ],
        "children": []
    },
...
```

Next, with this information you now know that if you wanted to run a playbook against the utility container, all you would have to do is execute the playbook like this:

```
$ ansible-playbook -i inventory/dynamic_inventory.py playbooks/base.yml
-l utility_container
```

Summary

Let's pause here on exploring the dynamic inventory script capabilities and continue to build upon it as we dissect the working examples in the next chapters.

Personally, I am very excited to move to the next chapter where we will create our very first OpenStack administration playbook together. We will start off with a fairly simple task of creating users and tenants. This will also include reviewing a few automation considerations, which you will need to remember while creating automation code for OpenStack. Ready? Ok, let's get started!

3
Creating Multiple Users/Tenants

We have finally arrived at the part of the book where we can put our hands on the keyboard and create our very first OpenStack administration playbook. The task of creating users and tenants for your OpenStack cloud is literally one of the first steps in setting up your cloud for user consumption. So, let's get started. We will see how one would manually do this first and then transition into creating a playbook with roles to fully automate it. While creating the playbook/role, I will try to highlight any possible concerns and flexible ways in which you can accomplish this using Ansible. We will cover the following:

- Creating users and tenants
- Automation considerations
- Coding the playbook and roles
- The playbook and role review

Creating users and tenants

Creating new users and tenants seems like a simple task for a cloud operator/administrator, but it does become a burden if asked to create 10, 20, or 50 users and 5, 10, or 20 tenants. First, we create the user (with a corresponding complex secure password), we then create the tenant for the user, and finally, we link that user to that tenant while assigning that user the appropriate role.

Imagine doing this over and over again. Boring! The first thing you learn as an administrator of anything is *figure out what your daily tasks are and then determine how to get them completed as fast/easily as possible*. This is exactly what we are going to do here.

Manually creating users and tenants

To further demonstrate the steps outlined earlier, we will walk you through the commands used to create a user and tenant.

 For simplicity purposes, we will demonstrate the manual commands using the OpenStack CLI only.

Creating a user

Creating a user within OpenStack involves sending requests to the Identity service (Keystone). The Keystone request can be executed by either first sourcing the OpenRC file, as discussed in *Chapter 1, An Introduction to OpenStack*, or by passing authentication parameters in line with the command (this is shown in the second example). Next, you will be responsible for providing the required parameter values, such as the username and password with the command. Let's take a look at the following example:

```
$ source openrc
$ keystone user-create --name=<username> --pass=<password>
```

Or we can also use this command:

```
$ keystone --os-username=<OS_USERNAME> --os-password=<OS_PASSWORD> --os-tenant-name=<OS_TENANT_NAME> --os-auth-url=<OS_AUTH_URL> user-create --name=<username> --pass=<password>
```

The output will look similar to this:

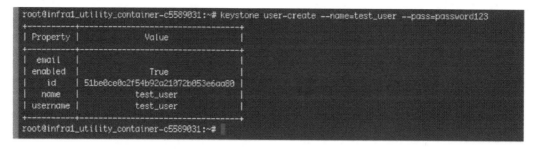

Creating a tenant

As mentioned previously, a tenant (also known as a project in current versions of OpenStack) is a segregated area of your cloud where you can assign users. The user can be restricted to just that tenant or it can be allowed access to multiple tenants. The process of creating a tenant is similar to the user creation process mentioned earlier. You can continue to execute CLI commands once you source the OpenRC file or pass authentication parameters with each command. Imagine that the OpenRC file has already been sourced, as shown in the following example:

```
$ keystone tenant-create --name=<tenant name> --description="<tenant
description>"
```

The output would look similar to this:

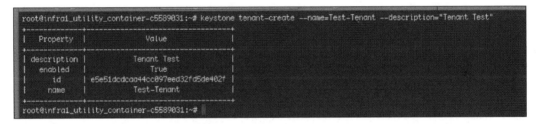

Assigning users role and tenant access

Using the keystone service, you can assign a specific role (user permissions) to a designated tenant for the user that you just created. There are default roles that come with a base OpenStack cloud: `admin and _member_`. You can also create custom roles as well. You will need the name of the role and tenant that you wish to assign to the user. If the OpenRC file is still sourced, refer to the following example:

```
$ keystone user-role-add --user=<username> --tenant=<tenant name>
--role=<role name>
```

At this point, you will have created a user and tenant and assigned that user to the tenant with a role; this is all done manually. Let's move forward to review some of the considerations around the thought of automating all the steps, as mentioned earlier.

Automation considerations

The idea of taking a manual task and creating an automation script, no matter the automation tool, requires some base framework decisions to be made. This is to keep consistency within your code and allow the easy adoption of your code by someone else. Ever tried using scripts created by someone else who had no code standards? It is confusing, and you waste a lot of time attempting to understand their approach.

In our case, we are going to make some framework decisions ahead of time and keep this consistency. My biggest disclaimer before we get started with reviewing the considerations in order to set our framework decisions is as follows:

 There are many ways to approach automating tasks for OpenStack with Ansible. The one shown in this book is just one of the ways I personally have found success with, and it's most certainly not the only way. The playbooks/roles are intended to be working examples, so you can use as is or adjust/improve for your personal use cases.

Now that this has been said, let's get on with it.

Defining variables globally or per role

This topic may not seem important enough to be reviewed, but in reality, with Ansible, you have more options than usual. With that thought, you will have to decide how you will define your variables within the roles.

Ansible has a variable definition hierarchy that it follows. You have the option to define the value of a variable placed within your playbook/role globally, or assign it to a group of hosts or locals for that specific role only. Defining the value globally would mean that all playbooks/roles can use this value and apply it to a group of hosts. If you set the value locally to that role, only that role would have access to the variable value.

Globally defined variable values will be defined in a file located in the group_vars/ directory of the playbook. The filename will have to match a group name set in the hosts file. To recap this process, refer to *Chapter 2, An Introduction to Ansible*, under the *Defining variable values* section. The advantage of this approach is that you can set the variable value once and have your playbooks/roles just reuse the value. This simplifies the process of defining variables overall and the tasks of updating the values as needed. On the other hand the disadvantage of this approach is you cannot reuse a variable name and provide a different value on a per role basis. This is where the alternative option comes into play.

Defining the variable value locally to the role allows the reuse of a variable name and the capability to define different values for that variable. Through my experience of creating playbooks/roles against an OpenStack cloud, I have found that defining the variables locally to a role seems to be the best option. My overall approach to creating roles is to create roles that are as simple as possible and that accomplish a single administrative task. Try not to combine multiple administrative tasks into a single role. Keeping the role simple enables the ability to reuse the role and be in line with Ansible's best practices.

So, the first framework decision that we make here is we define variable values locally to the role. Now, we can move on to the next consideration/decision point, which is whether to use the OpenStack API or CLI to execute administrative commands.

The OpenStack API or CLI

Again, this decision may seem unimportant at a high level. Deciding whether to use the OpenStack API or CLI could drastically change the overall structure and approach to creating your playbooks/roles. In Chapter 1, *An Introduction to OpenStack*, we covered the difference between the OpenStack API and CLI.

One thing that stands out is that the CLI is much easier to use and code than Ansible. Keep in mind that the CLI still executes API commands behind the scenes, dealing with all the token and JSON interpretation stuff for you. This allows zero loss in the functionality.

The second framework decision that we make is we create roles to make calls to your OpenStack cloud using the CLI commands. With this decision, we then need to standardize the way in which we will authorize each CLI command. While I would like to say that I am not a fan of adding extra syntaxes to commands, this by far outweighs the alternative of making API calls in the automation code.

For each CLI command, you will find the following authorization strings with defined variables:

```
--os-username={{ OS_USERNAME }} --os-password={{ OS_PASSWORD }} --os-
tenant-name={{ OS_TENANT_NAME }} --os-auth-url={{ OS_AUTH_URL }}
```

The good news is that these variables are the only variables defined as global variables, and they only need to be updated in one place. Now, we need to decide from where do we wish to execute the playbooks.

Where to run Ansible

My next statement may be a bit obvious, but the playbooks need to be executed from a workstation/server with Ansible installed. Now that we have this out of the way, let's explore our options:

- I would recommend that you do not run the playbooks directly from any of the OpenStack controller nodes. The controller nodes have plenty of work to do in order to just keep OpenStack going, so no need to add an additional burden.

- The other option is to execute the playbooks from some sort of centralized Ansible server in your environment. While this is a totally viable option, I have one better for you.

Since I am a huge fan and advocate of the **OpenStack Ansible Deployment** (OSAD) method of deploying OpenStack, the playbooks/roles out of the box will use some of the great features offered by OSAD. My last sentence may seem a bit off topic, but it will make more sense shortly.

One of the greatest features that comes with running OSAD is the built-in dynamic inventory script. This feature removes your burden of keeping the inventory of your OpenStack service locations in a `hosts` file. In order to benefit from this feature, you will need to execute the playbooks/roles from the OSAD deployment server, which in the big picture it makes sense to keep all the Ansible playbooks/roles together (deployment and administration scripts).

The other compelling reason why this is the best option is that the OSAD deployment server is already set up to communicate with the LXC containers, where the OpenStack services are located. This point is very important when/if you want to make OpenStack service configuration changes to Ansible.

The last feature of OSAD that I would like to highlight is the fact that it comes with a container designated just to administer your OpenStack cloud, called the **utility** container. This container comes with every OpenStack service CLI package installed. Yes, one less thing for you to worry about. This is why I love OSAD.

Our last framework decision that we make is we execute the playbooks from the OSAD deployment server in order to take full advantage of all the features OSAD offers us (it just feels right). Now that we are all armed with tons of good information and coding framework, all we have to do is create our first playbook and roles.

Coding the playbook and roles

Before we start, we should first refer to the beginning of this chapter. We outlined the steps to create users and tenants within your OpenStack cloud. Here they are again for a quick reference:

- Creating the user (with a corresponding complex secure password)
- Creating the tenant for the user
- Linking the user to the tenant while assigning that user with the appropriate role

The first step is to tackle the user creation portion of the process. Creating a user is a simple task in OpenStack, so why not add some administration flares to go along with it. Part of the process of creating a user is to assign that user an appropriate password. We will include this as part of the role that creates the user and tenant that we will assign the user to.

When creating a playbook, I normally start with creating roles to handle the administrative tasks needed. The role will contain all the executable code against OpenStack cloud. The playbook will contain the host to run the role against (in this case, the *utility* container) the role(s) to be executed and other execution settings. The role to handle this administrative task will be named `create-users-env`.

The directory structure of our playbook will look like this:

```
base.yml                 # master playbook for user creation
group_vars/
    util_container       # assign variable values for this host group
hosts                    # static host inventory file
roles/
    create-users-env     # user/tenant creation role
        tasks/
            main.yml     # tasks file for this role
        vars/
            main.yml     # variables associated with this role
```

Since we will start with the role task file assembly, let's create the `main.yml` file in the `create-users-env/tasks` directory. The contents at the beginning of this file will look like this:

```
---

- name: Install random password generator package
  apt: name={{item}} state=present
  with_items:
```

```
    - apg

  - name: Random generate passwords
    command: apg -n {{ pass_cnt }} -M NCL -q
    register: passwdss

  - name: Create users
    command: keystone --os-username={{ OS_USERNAME }} --os-password={{
OS_PASSWORD }} --os-tenant-name={{ OS_TENANT_NAME }} --os-auth-url={{
OS_AUTH_URL }}
             user-create --name={{ item.0 }} --pass={{ item.1 }}
    with_together:
      - userid
      - passwdss.stdout_lines
```

Now, we can go through the three tasks that were just added to the role, as
mentioned previously, in more detail. The first task sets the groundwork to
use the apg package, which generates several random passwords, as shown
in the following code:

```
  - name: Install random password generator package
    apt: name={{item}} state=present
    with_items:
      - apg
```

Since in the second task, we will use the apg package to generate passwords for us,
we need to make sure that it is installed on the host that executes the playbook/role.
The apt module from Ansible is a very useful tool used to manage Debian/Ubuntu
packages. Defining the {{item}} parameter value with the module allows us to loop
through multiple packages listed in the with_items statement. In this particular
case, it is not needed as we are only installing one package, but at the same time,
does us no harm. Moving on to the second task:

```
  - name: Random generate passwords
    command: apg -n {{ pass_cnt }} -M NCL -q
    register: passwdss
```

The second task will execute the apg package using the command module
from Ansible.

> The command module is one of the most commonly used modules when
> working with Ansible. Basically, it can handle the execution of any
> command/package with the exception of any commands that will utilize
> shell variables and shell specific operations, such as: <, >, |, and &.

With the `command` module, we pass the `apg` command with specific parameters, such as `-n {{ pass_cnt }} -M NCL -q`. Most of the parameters are standard options for `apg`, with the exception of the `{{ pass_cnt }}` variable. Setting this parameter allows us to adjust the number of passwords generated from the variable file set for this role (found in the `create-users-env/vars` directory). We will examine the variable file shortly. One of the last steps in this task is to register the output of the `apg` command into a variable named `passwdss`. This variable will be used later in this role.

The third task that is added to the role will now create the user in your OpenStack cloud. As shown in the following code, using the `command` module, we will execute the keystone command to create a user with authentication parameters:

```
- name: Create users
  command: keystone --os-username={{ OS_USERNAME }} --os-password={{
OS_PASSWORD }} --os-tenant-name={{ OS_TENANT_NAME }} --os-auth-url={{
OS_AUTH_URL }}
          user-create --name={{ item.0 }} --pass={{ item.1 }}
  with_together:
    - userid
    - passwdss.stdout_lines
```

In the `user-create` command, we will also define a few variables that can be used:

```
{{ item.0 }}   # variable placeholder used to set the usernames from
the list defined in the userid variable

{{ item.1 }}   # variable placeholder used to read in the output from
the apg command found within the passwdss variable registered earlier
```

> Placing variables in your commands sets you up for creating roles with core code that you will not have to update every time it is used. A much simpler process is to just update variable files instead of continuously altering role tasks.

The other special part of this task is the use of the `with_together` Ansible loop command. This command allows us to loop through separate sets of variable values, pairing them together in the defined order. Since the passwords are random, we need not care about what user gets which password.

So, now that we have our user creation code in the role, the next step is to create the user's tenant. The following two tasks are as follows:

```
- name: Create user environments
  command: keystone --os-username={{ OS_USERNAME }} --os-password={{
OS_PASSWORD }} --os-tenant-name={{ OS_TENANT_NAME }} --os-auth-url={{
OS_AUTH_URL }}
          tenant-create --name={{ item }} --description="{{ item }}"
  with_items: tenantid

- name: Assign user to specified role in designated environment
  command: keystone --os-username={{ OS_USERNAME }} --os-password={{
OS_PASSWORD }} --os-tenant-name={{ OS_TENANT_NAME }} --os-auth-url={{
OS_AUTH_URL }}
          user-role-add --user={{ item.0 }} --tenant={{ item.1 }}
--role={{ urole }}
  with_together:
    - userid
    - tenantid
```

The first preceding task will create the tenant with the `tenant-create` keystone command. The tenant name and description will come from the `tenantid` variable. The next task, as mentioned previously, will then assign the user that we created earlier to this newly created tenant with a role value set by the `urole` variable.

You will notice that these tasks are very similar to the previous tasks that were used to create the user, and they also use similar Ansible parameters. Again here we will use the `command` module to execute the keystone commands with variable placeholders. As you can see, it will begin to form a repeated pattern. This really helps the code creation.

The last task of the role will simply provide an output of the users created and their corresponding passwords. This step will give you (as the Cloud operator) a very simple output with all the information that you would need to save and/or pass on to the Cloud consumer. While this step is not required to complete the overall administrative task, it is nice to have it.

Let's take a look at the following task:

```
- name: User password assignment
  debug: msg="User {{ item.0 }} was added to {{ item.2 }} tenant, with
the assigned password of {{ item.1 }}"
  with_together:
    - userid
    - passwdss.stdout_lines
    - tenantid
```

In this task, we will use the `debug` module to show the output of the variable that we set either manually or dynamically using the `register` Ansible command. The output will look something like this:

```
TASK: [create-users-env | User password assignment] *******************************
ok: [172.29.236.199] => (item=['mrkt-dev01', u'edribSov7', 'MRKT-Proj01']) => {
    "item": [
        "mrkt-dev01",
        "edribSov7",
        "MRKT-Proj01"
    ],
    "msg": "User mrkt-dev01 was added to MRKT-Proj01 tenant, with the assigned password of edribSov7"
}
ok: [172.29.236.199] => (item=['mrkt-dev02', u'wiowWef0', 'MRKT-Proj02']) => {
    "item": [
        "mrkt-dev02",
        "wiowWef0",
        "MRKT-Proj02"
    ],
    "msg": "User mrkt-dev02 was added to MRKT-Proj02 tenant, with the assigned password of wiowWef0"
}
ok: [172.29.236.199] => (item=['mrkt-dev03', u'PhiodCoup9', 'MRKT-Proj03']) => {
    "item": [
        "mrkt-dev03",
        "PhiodCoup9",
        "MRKT-Proj03"
    ],
    "msg": "User mrkt-dev03 was added to MRKT-Proj03 tenant, with the assigned password of PhiodCoup9"
}
```

Believe it or not, you have just created your first OpenStack administration role. To support this role, we now need to create the variable file that will go along with it. The `main.yml` variable filename, located in the `create-users-env/vars` directory, is very similar to the task file in structure.

> Keep in mind that the values defined in the variable file are intended to be changed before each execution for normal everyday use.

The values shown in the following example are just working examples. Let's take a look at them:

```
---
pass_cnt: 10
userid: [ 'mrkt-dev01', 'mrkt-dev02', 'mrkt-dev03', 'mrkt-dev04',
'mrkt-dev05', 'mrkt-dev06', 'mrkt-dev07', 'mrkt-dev08', 'mrkt-dev09',
'mrkt-dev10' ]
tenantid: [ 'MRKT-Proj01', 'MRKT-Proj02', 'MRKT-Proj03', 'MRKT-
Proj04', 'MRKT-Proj05', 'MRKT-Proj06', 'MRKT-Proj07', 'MRKT-Proj08',
'MRKT-Proj09', 'MRKT-Proj10' ]
urole: _member_
```

Let's take a moment to break down each variable. The summary will be as follows:

```
pass_cnt    # with the value of 10, we would be creating 10 random
passwords with apg

userid      # the value is a comma delimited list of users to loop thru
when executing the user-create Keystone command

tenanted    # the value is a comma delimited list of tenant names to
loop thru when executing the tenant-create Keystone command

urole       # with the value of _member_, the user would be assigned
the member role to the tenant created
```

This pretty much concludes what is involved when creating a variable file. We can now move on to the base of this playbook and create the master playbook file named base.yml, which is located in the root of the playbook directory. The contents of the base.yml file will be as follows:

```
---

# This playbook used to demo OpenStack Juno user, role and tenant
features.

- hosts: util_container
  user: root
  remote_user: root
  sudo: yes
  roles:
- create-users-env
```

The summary of this file is as follows:

```
hosts        # the host or host group to execute the playbook against

user         # the user to use when executing the playbook locally

remote_user  # the user to use when executing the playbook on the
remote host(s)

sudo         # will tell Ansible to sudo into the above user on the
remote host(s)

roles        # provide a list of roles to execute as part of this
playbook
```

The last two areas that we need to focus on before we complete the playbook and make it ready for execution are to create the host inventory file and the global variable file. In this case, we are using a static host inventory file to keep things simple, but in future chapters, we will instead use the OSAD dynamic inventory file. As we are using the static inventory file, we will have to discover the name and/or IP address of the *utility* container.

This can be accomplished by running the following command on any of the controller nodes:

```
$ lxc-ls -fancy
```

Then, we look for something similar to the highlighted item in the output:

Then, add the *utility* container's IP address to the `hosts` file, as follows:

```
[localhost]
localhost ansible_connection=local

[util_container]
172.29.236.199
```

Last but not least, you will create the global variable file inside the `group_vars/` directory. Remember that the file must be named to match the host or host group defined in the master playbook. Since we called the `util_container` host group, we must then name the variable file with the exact same name. The contents of the `util_container` global variable file will be as follows:

```
# Here are variables related globally to the util_container host group

OS_USERNAME: ansible
OS_PASSWORD: passwd
OS_TENANT_NAME: admin
OS_AUTH_URL: http://172.29.236.7:35357/v2.0
```

ProTip

Always create/use an automation service account when executing commands against a system remotely. Never use the built-in admin and/ or your personal account for that system. The use of service accounts is useful for simple troubleshooting and system audits.

You will recall that, earlier in this chapter, we spoke about the authorization string needed to use the CLI commands. Here they are again as a reminder:

```
--os-username={{ OS_USERNAME }} --os-password={{ OS_PASSWORD }} --os-
tenant-name={{ OS_TENANT_NAME }} --os-auth-url={{ OS_AUTH_URL }}
```

The variable placeholder that we set in the roles task file relates back to this global variable file. This is where the values for the variables that we set are stored.

A word of caution

Due to the contents of this file, it should be stored as a secure file in whatever code repository you may use to store your Ansible playbooks/ roles. Gaining access to this information can compromise your OpenStack cloud security.

Guess what, you made it! We just completely finished our first OpenStack administration playbook and role. Let's finish this chapter with a quick overview of the playbook and role that we just created.

The playbook and role review

To get started, we can start from the top with the role we created called
create-users-env. The completed role and file named main.yml is located
in the create-users-env/tasks directory, which looks like this:

```
---

- name: Install random password generator package
  apt: name={{item}} state=present
  with_items:
    - apg

- name: Random generate passwords
  command: apg -n {{ pass_cnt }} -M NCL -q
  register: passwdss

- name: Create users
  command: keystone --os-username={{ OS_USERNAME }} --os-password={{
OS_PASSWORD }} --os-tenant-name={{ OS_TENANT_NAME }} --os-auth-url={{
OS_AUTH_URL }}
          user-create --name={{ item.0 }} --pass={{ item.1 }}
  with_together:
    - userid
    - passwdss.stdout_lines

- name: Create user environments
  command: keystone --os-username={{ OS_USERNAME }} --os-password={{
OS_PASSWORD }} --os-tenant-name={{ OS_TENANT_NAME }} --os-auth-url={{
OS_AUTH_URL }}
          tenant-create --name={{ item }} --description="{{ item }}"
  with_items: tenantid

- name: Assign user to specified role in designated environment
  command: keystone --os-username={{ OS_USERNAME }} --os-password={{
OS_PASSWORD }} --os-tenant-name={{ OS_TENANT_NAME }} --os-auth-url={{
OS_AUTH_URL }}
          user-role-add --user={{ item.0 }} --tenant={{ item.1 }}
--role={{ urole }}
  with_together:
    - userid
    - tenantid
```

```
- name: User password assignment
  debug: msg="User {{ item.0 }} was added to {{ item.2 }} tenant, with
the assigned password of {{ item.1 }}"
  with_together:
    - userid
    - passwdss.stdout_lines
    - tenantid
```

The corresponding variable file named `main.yml`, located in the `create-users-env/` `vars` directory, for this role will look like this:

```
---
pass_cnt: 10
userid: [ 'mrkt-dev01', 'mrkt-dev02', 'mrkt-dev03', 'mrkt-dev04',
'mrkt-dev05', 'mrkt-dev06', 'mrkt-dev07', 'mrkt-dev08', 'mrkt-dev09',
'mrkt-dev10' ]
tenantid: [ 'MRKT-Proj01', 'MRKT-Proj02', 'MRKT-Proj03', 'MRKT-
Proj04', 'MRKT-Proj05', 'MRKT-Proj06', 'MRKT-Proj07', 'MRKT-Proj08',
'MRKT-Proj09', 'MRKT-Proj10' ]
urole: _member_
```

Next, the master playbook file named `base.yml`, located in the root of the playbook directory, will look like this:

```
---
# This playbook used to demo OpenStack Juno user, role and tenant
features.

- hosts: util_container
  user: root
  remote_user: root
  sudo: yes
  roles:
- create-users-env
```

Following this, we created the `hosts` file, which is also located in the root of the playbook directory:

```
[localhost]
localhost ansible_connection=local

[util_container]
172.29.236.199
```

Lastly, we wrapped this playbook by creating the global variable file named `util_container` and saving it to the `group_vars/` directory of the playbook:

```
# Here are variables related globally to the util_container host group

OS_USERNAME: ansible
OS_PASSWORD: passwd
OS_TENANT_NAME: admin
OS_AUTH_URL: http://172.29.236.7:35357/v2.0
```

As promised earlier, I felt it was very important to provide fully working Ansible playbooks and roles for your consumption. You can use them as is and/or as a springboard to create new/improved Ansible code. The code can be found in the GitHub repository available at `https://github.com/os-admin-with-ansible/os-admin-with-ansible`.

Now, of course, we have to test our work. Assuming that you have cloned the preceding GitHub repository, the command to test the playbook from the deployment node will be as follows:

```
$ cd os-admin-with-ansible
$ ansible-playbook -i hosts base.yml
```

Summary

See, now that was not so bad right? Ansible really does a great job in streamlining the efforts involved in automating OpenStack administrative tasks. You can now reuse that role over and over again, reducing the amount of time required to create users and tenants to single digit minutes. The time investment is well worth the benefits.

We covered how to create users and tenants in OpenStack via the API and CLI, gathered an understanding of basic automation considerations, and developed the Ansible playbook and role to automate the user and tenant creation.

With this great foundation, we are ready to move on to our next administrative task of customizing your cloud quotas. The next chapter will include a general understanding of what quotas are and how they are used in your OpenStack cloud. We will then transition into the exercise of creating quotas manually and then conclude with how to automate tasks with Ansible. See you in *Chapter 4, Customizing Your Cloud's Quotas.*

4
Customizing Your Cloud's Quotas

Now that we have tackled creating our first OpenStack administration playbook, it is time to move on to our next task. The next task will cover the method to customize the tenant quotas in your cloud. This is normally the next step in the process of setting up new projects/tenants for your cloud consumers. First, we will see how we can do this manually and then transition into creating a playbook with roles, to fully automate it. In this chapter, we will cover the following topics:

- Define and create quotas
- Automation considerations
- Coding the playbook and roles
- Playbook and role review

Define and create quotas

What are **quotas**? Within OpenStack, you can set quotas on a tenant/project or user level in order to restrict the resource consumption that is allowed. The compute service (Nova) manages the quota values and also enforces them. As a cloud operator, this is another important feature OpenStack offers, as quotas allow you to control the cloud's overall system capacity. You may ask, why not just set up one default quota and let every tenant use it? We will cover why this approach may or may not work, based on a particular use case. It is also worth mentioning that the Block Storage service (Cinder) can also set quotas.

Since we now know that you can set quotas, let's review the resources that can be restricted and what the default values are. The following is a table describing the type of quotas that can be set:

Quota name	Defines the number of...
Instances	Instances allowed for each project
Cores	Instance cores allowed for each project
RAM (MB)	RAM megabytes allowed for each instance
Floating IPs	Floating IPs allowed for each project
Fixed IPs	Fixed IPs allowed for each project
Metadata items	Metadata items allowed for each instance
Injected files	Injected files allowed for each project
Injected file content bytes	Content bytes allowed for each injected file
Keypairs	Keypairs allowed for each project
Security groups	Security groups allowed for each project
Security group rules	Rules allowed for each security group
Server groups	Server groups allowed for each project
Server group members	Server group members allowed for each project

As you can see, there are quite a few options to apply restrictions to. As a cloud operator, you might want to take full advantage of tuning these options on a per tenant basis. Taking this approach allows you to optimize your cloud usage; in essence, it stretches your resources further while provisioning only what is needed. As an administrator, I hated seeing wasted resources hanging out there that could be used for something else, if better controls were in place. In this case quotas serve a bit of the opposite purpose, as they are put in place to avoid the cloud consumer from exhausting all of the cloud resources.

Yes, the process of tuning quotas involves effort (aka extra work) and this is why the concept of setting global default quota values has become popular. To view the default quota values, you will have to execute the following command:

```
$ nova quota-show
```

The output will look similar to this:

```
root@infra1_utility_container-c750da76:~# nova quota-show
+-----------------------------+--------+
| Quota                       | Limit  |
+-----------------------------+--------+
| instances                   | 10     |
| cores                       | 20     |
| ram                         | 51200  |
| floating_ips                | 10     |
| fixed_ips                   | -1     |
| metadata_items              | 128    |
| injected_files              | 5      |
| injected_file_content_bytes | 10240  |
| injected_file_path_bytes    | 255    |
| key_pairs                   | 100    |
| security_groups             | 10     |
| security_group_rules        | 20     |
| server_groups               | 10     |
| server_group_members        | 10     |
+-----------------------------+--------+
```

 Whenever you wish to set a quota value to be unlimited, set the value to
-1. This tells Nova to allow that resource to be unrestricted for that tenant
or globally, if set as default.

Now, let's focus on how we can adjust the quota values manually, using the CLI.
For simplicity purposes we will demonstrate the manual commands using the
OpenStack CLI only.

Creating quotas manually

To be accurate, you only have the capability to update the values set for global
quotas or quotas set for a specific tenant/project. You cannot create new quotas
to just update the values. The listing, updating, and resetting of a quota involves
sending requests to the compute service (Nova).

Just like with every OpenStack service, you must authenticate either by sourcing
the OpenRC file discussed in *Chapter 1, An Introduction to OpenStack*, or by passing
authentication parameters in line with the command. You will then need to provide
the values for the quota you wish to update (refer to the preceding table for your
options). Now, let's look at the following example:

```
$ source openrc
$ nova quota-update --instances=<value> --cores=<value><tenant id>
```

Or, you can also use:

```
$ nova --os-username=<OS_USERNAME> --os-password=<OS_PASSWORD>  --os-
tenant-name=<OS_TENANT_NAME> --os-auth-url=<OS_AUTH_URL> quota-update
--instances=<value> --cores=<value><tenant id>
```

No output is written on the screen once the command is executed. You can then execute the quota-show command to confirm the update.

A real-life working example might look something like this:

```
$ nova quota-update –instances=100 –cores=50
903127b0aae141f298ffacf2cf8394dc
```

The output of the quota-show command will then be:

```
root@infra1_utility_container-c750da76:~# nova quota-show
+-----------------------------+--------+
| Quota                       | Limit  |
+-----------------------------+--------+
| instances                   | 100    |
| cores                       | 50     |
| ram                         | 51200  |
| floating_ips                | 10     |
| fixed_ips                   | -1     |
| metadata_items              | 128    |
| injected_files              | 5      |
| injected_file_content_bytes | 10240  |
| injected_file_path_bytes    | 255    |
| key_pairs                   | 100    |
| security_groups             | 10     |
| security_group_rules        | 20     |
| server_groups               | 10     |
| server_group_members        | 10     |
+-----------------------------+--------+
```

Note that the above example only shows updating the *instance* and *core* quota for a tenant. There are other quota values that can be updated.

Setting up default quotas

In the event you wish to set up a default quota that all tenants/projects and users will be assigned to, the process is a bit different. Nova also manages the default quota assignments. Setting up a default quota can be very useful when you wish to create a tenant/project or user with automatic built-in controls in place.

Nothing is worse than creating a tenant that has no resource restrictions, and before you know it the consumers of that tenant exhausts your cloud space. The cloud is intended to give consumers the impression of it being limitless. In reality, we all know that there is no such thing; everything has a limit of some manner. From my experience, if you give a user a 20 vCPU they will use it all if allowed. Putting cloud resource restrictions in place are very important as a cloud operator.

The command to update the default quota for your cloud is as shown. This command can be executed after authenticating it just as the preceding the examples. The quota options are the same as updating a tenant or user specific quota. Again, please refer to the preceding table for your options. Here is an example:

```
$ nova quota-class-update --ram=<value> --security-groups=<value><quota class name>
```

One of the main differences with the above command is you must supply something that Nova refers to as a **quota class**. A quota class is the way Nova distinguishes between a default quota and a custom quota you may set up. Assuming future releases of Nova will include the ability to create additional quota classes. For now, you only have the ability to update the only quota class available, which is named `default`.

A working example of the command will look like this:

```
$ nova quota-class-update --ram=-1 --security-groups=30 default
```

The output of the `quota-class-show` command will then be:

```
root@infra1_utility_container-c750da76:~# nova quota-class-show default
+-----------------------------+-------+
| Quota                       | Limit |
+-----------------------------+-------+
| instances                   | 10    |
| cores                       | 20    |
| ram                         | -1    |
| floating_ips                | 10    |
| fixed_ips                   | -1    |
| metadata_items              | 128   |
| injected_files              | 5     |
| injected_file_content_bytes | 10240 |
| injected_file_path_bytes    | 255   |
| key_pairs                   | 100   |
| security_groups             | 30    |
| security_group_rules        | 20    |
| server_groups               | 10    |
| server_group_members        | 10    |
+-----------------------------+-------+
```

Please keep in mind, whatever you set the default quota values to will be what every tenant or user will configure initially.

Reset quota values

A time might come when you may want to start fresh and reset a quota set for a tenant(s) or user(s). Fortunately this is an easy process within OpenStack. You will use the `quota-delete` command for Nova. This will delete the custom quota and reset it back to the default quota, as shown in the following example:

```
$ nova quota-delete --tenant=<tenant-id> [--user=<user-id>]
```

With the preceding command, you can supply either the tenant ID or the user ID in which you want to revert the quota back to the default values.

Automation considerations

While creating this role there was only one automation decision that I had to make outside of the ones we covered in the previous chapter. All the other considerations carried over.

Since the Nova quota commands allow for numerous options to be passed with no inter-dependencies, we have to figure out a way to not restrict that flexibility in the role and at the same time not require constant updates directly to the role. Ansible makes such a decision really easy by allow for variables to be passed as a hash. Within the variables file you can then define the options for each tenant or user and have the task cycle through each tenant/user with those options.

 I promise this is the last time I will make this disclaimer but, I felt it is important to emphasize. There are many ways to approach automating tasks for OpenStack with Ansible; the one shown in this book is one way I personally have found success with and most certainly not the only way. The playbooks/roles are intended to be working examples that you can use as is or adjust/improve for your personal use cases.

Similar to last time, now that this has been said, let's get on with creating this role.

Coding the playbook and roles

We will now create a role that allows us to update a single and/or multiple tenant(s) quota at one time. Updating a quota is a relatively simple two-step process. Step 1 is to record the tenant ID or user ID, in which you wish to update the quota. Then step 2 is to actually update the quota.

Since we are only creating a role in this example, we can start with the `main.yml` file within the role directory named `adjust-quotas/tasks`. The initial contents of this file will look similar to the following code:

```
---

- name: Retrieve tenantID
  shell: keystone --os-username={{ OS_USERNAME }} --os-password={{ OS_
PASSWORD }} --os-tenant-name={{ OS_TENANT_NAME }} --os-auth-url={{
OS_AUTH_URL }}
  tenant-list | awk '/ {{ item }} / { print $2 }'
  with_items: tenantname
  register: tenantid
```

The first step of pulling the tenant ID is simple and straightforward with the use of the `awk` command and pipe (|) symbol. This approach is something you will see in a lot of the OpenStack documentation. It enables you to take the output of one command and filter out the parts you want to keep.

First, we will execute the `tenant-list` command; the output will then be used with a filter and the filter will search for the tenant name provided via the variable named `tenantname`; and finally, it will output the second column value from the original `tenant-list` command. The final output will then be registered with the variable named `tenantid`. Later in the chapter, we will explore the method to define the `tenantname` variable.

As seen in the previous chapter, defining the `{{item}}` parameter value with the module allows us to loop through the multiple packages listed inside the `with_items` statement.

> The `shell` module will be the second most used module when working with Ansible. It behaves just like the command module, but it also interprets shell variables and shell specific operations such as: <, >, |, and &.

The use of the `shell` module here is due to executing commands that are needed to get the tenant ID.

The next task will now do the actual quota update. The code to accomplish this looks similar to the following code block:

```
- name: Adjust tenant quotas
command: nova --os-username={{ OS_USERNAME }} --os-password={{ OS_
PASSWORD }} --os-tenant-name={{ OS_TENANT_NAME }} --os-auth-url={{
OS_AUTH_URL }}
quota-update {{ item.0 }} {{ item.1.stdout }}
with_together:
    - qoptions
    - tenantid.results
```

Just like the manual commands that we reviewed earlier in this chapter, you must supply the quota options you wish to adjust and the tenant ID registered earlier in the variable `tenantid`. Again, we are using the `with_together` command to loop through the two variables defined by pairing the values together.

Here is a further breakdown of the variables defined in the preceding task:

```
{{ item.0 }}   # variable placeholder used to set the quota options to
update
```

```
{{ item.1.stdout }}   # variable placeholder used to read in the
output from the filtered tenant-list command found within the tenantid
variable registered earlier
```

The `{{ item.1.stdout }}` variable placeholder is defined uniquely due to the way the output is stored within the variable's JSON data structure.

ProTip

Finding how a variable's output is defined within the JSON data structure is probably the only annoying and time consuming thing I can think of with Ansible. Honestly, it is not Ansible's fault, it just gets a bad wrap. To avoid this unrequired annoyance you can use the `debug` module before further coding the role to use that variable. Do not be shy about this, as this will give you an idea of how you will have to define the placeholder.

When the role is executed, no output is generated in this particular case. If you want to provide an output to confirm the successful execution of the task, you can add the quota-show command as an additional task in your role. An example will look similar to this:

```
- name: Confirm tenant quota update
command: nova --os-username={{ OS_USERNAME }} --os-password={{ OS_
PASSWORD }} --os-tenant-name={{ OS_TENANT_NAME }} --os-auth-url={{
OS_AUTH_URL }}
quota-show {{ item.1.stdout }}
with_items: tenantid.results
```

You have now completed your second OpenStack administration role. To support this role, we now need to create the variable file that will go along with it. The variable file which is named main.yml will be located in the adjust-quotas/vars directory.

Note that the values defined in the variable file are intended to be changed before each execution, for normal everyday use.

The values shown in the following example are just working examples. Let's take a look:

```
---
qoptions: [ '--cores 30', '--instances 20 --cores 20', '--instances 20
--cores 20' ]
tenantname: [ 'MRKT-Proj01', 'MRKT-Proj02', 'MRKT-Proj03' ]
```

Let's take a moment to break down each variable. The summary will be:

```
qoptions # this is where you declare the quota options you wish to
update, each set of options and values are encapsulated within single
quotes comma delimited; there is no limit on the number of options
that can be added

tenantname # the value is a comma delimited list of tenant names you
wish to update quotas for
```

Now that our variable file is created, we can move on to creating the master playbook file. Just like in the previous chapter, the file will be named `quota-update.yml` and saved to the root of the `playbook` directory. The contents of the `quota-update.yml` file will be:

```
---
# This playbook used to demo OpenStack Juno quota updates.

- hosts: util_container
user: root
remote_user: root
sudo: yes
roles:
adjust-quotas
```

The summary of this file is as follows:

```
hosts          # the host or host group to execute the playbook against

user           # the user to use when executing the playbook locally

remote_user    # the user to use when executing the playbook on the
remote host(s)

sudo           # will tell Ansible to sudo into the above user on the
remote host(s)

roles          # provide a list of roles to execute as part of this
playbook
```

All that is left is to populate our host inventory file and the global variable file. Since we already created these in the last chapter, there is no need to repeat this process. The values defined earlier will remain the same. There is a quick recap of how those files are configured in the following section.

The `hosts` file in the root of the `playbook` directory is as follows:

```
[localhost]
localhostansible_connection=local

[util_container]
172.29.236.199
```

The global variable file inside the `group_vars/` directory is as follows:

```
# Here are variables related globally to the util_container host group

OS_USERNAME: ansible
OS_PASSWORD: passwd
OS_TENANT_NAME: admin
OS_AUTH_URL: http://172.29.236.7:35357/v2.0
```

Word of caution

Due to the contents of this file, it should be stored as a secure file within the code repository that you may use to store your Ansible playbooks/roles. Gaining access to this information can compromise your OpenStack cloud security.

Okay, so here we have completed two administration playbooks and roles. As always, we will finish the chapter with a quick review of the playbook and the role just created.

Playbook and role review

To get to it right away, we can start from the top with the role we created, called `create-users-env`. The completed role and the file named `main.yml` is located in the `adjust-quotas/tasks` directory and it looks similar to the following code:

```
---

- name: Retrieve tenantID
shell: keystone --os-username={{ OS_USERNAME }} --os-password={{ OS_
PASSWORD }} --os-tenant-name={{ OS_TENANT_NAME }} --os-auth-url={{
OS_AUTH_URL }}
tenant-list | awk '/ {{ item }} / { print $2 }'
with_items: tenantname
register: tenantid

- name: Adjust tenant quotas
command: nova --os-username={{ OS_USERNAME }} --os-password={{ OS_
PASSWORD }} --os-tenant-name={{ OS_TENANT_NAME }} --os-auth-url={{
OS_AUTH_URL }}
quota-update {{ item.0 }} {{ item.1.stdout }}
with_together:
    - qoptions
    - tenantid.results
```

The corresponding variable file named `main.yml`, located in the `adjust-quota/vars` directory will look similar to this:

```
---
qoptions: [ '--cores 30', '--instances 20 --cores 20', '--instances 20
--cores 20' ]
tenantname: [ 'MRKT-Proj01', 'MRKT-Proj02', 'MRKT-Proj03' ]
```

Next, the master playbook file named `quota-update.yml`, located in the root of the `playbook` directory, will look similar to this:

```
---
# This playbook used to demo OpenStack Juno quota updates.

- hosts: util_container
user: root
remote_user: root
sudo: yes
roles:
adjust-quotas
```

Following that, we created the `hosts` file, which is also located in the root of the `playbook` directory:

```
[localhost]
localhostansible_connection=local

[util_container]
172.29.236.199
```

Lastly, we wrapped up this playbook by creating the global variable file named `util_container` and saving it to the `group_vars/` directory of the playbook:

```
# Here are variables related globally to the util_container host group

OS_USERNAME: ansible
OS_PASSWORD: passwd
OS_TENANT_NAME: admin
OS_AUTH_URL: http://172.29.236.7:35357/v2.0
```

 The complete set of code can again be found in the following GitHub repository https://github.com/os-admin-with-ansible/os-admin-with-ansible.

Now, of course we have to test our work. Assuming that you have cloned the GitHub repository in the preceding section, the command to test out the playbook from the deployment node will be as follows:

```
$ cd os-admin-with-ansible
$ ansible-playbook -i hosts quota-update.yml
```

Summary

Hopefully, by this point things are getting a bit easier to follow. You will notice that the steps to complete the playbooks/roles are similar despite the tasks themselves being different. Ansible is the key to simplifying those repeated steps. Just like in the last chapter, you can use this role in combination with others, as many times as you want. This is why you want to design your roles to be the base generic task, as much as possible.

Some of the things that we covered in this chapter were to define what a quota within OpenStack is. We then took that knowledge and learned how to update a quota for a tenant/user using the OpenStack CLI. We applied some base principles as to why you will use the default cloud quotas and how to update them appropriately. Next we reviewed how to reset any of the custom quotas created. Lastly, we developed our very own Ansible playbook and a role to automate the updating of custom tenant/user quotas.

Let's now move on to the next chapter, where we will take on the administrative task of snapshotting your cloud. The function of taking instance snapshots is a powerful tool if you want to use that instance as a gold copy and/or retain a backup of the instance. Understanding how to handle this sort of task on a cloud operator level is very beneficial. In the next chapter we will cover how to create snapshots manually, we will cover the power of being able to snapshot all instances within a tenant at once and then of course conclude with how to automate that task with Ansible. On to *Chapter 5, Snapshot Your Cloud* we go!

5
Snapshot Your Cloud

In this chapter, we will cover the task of creating instance backups and/or snapshots using the native OpenStack capability built into the compute service (Nova). When adopting a true cloud approach, you will find a great use in snapshots versus backups, but it is still a good idea to understand both the capabilities and the proper use case for each. We will see how to manually create backups or snapshots first and then move on to creating a playbook with roles to fully automate it on a tenant level. In this chapter, we will cover the following points:

- Define backups and snapshots
- Creating backups and snapshots manually
- Restoring an instance backup
- Automation considerations
- Coding the playbook and roles
- Playbook and role review

Define backups and snapshots

From an OpenStack perspective, there are distinct differences between a backup and a snapshot of an instance. Those differences could influence the use of each of those functions. Note that keeping with true cloud behavior, all cloud resources are meant to be disposable. You may ask, what does that statement really mean? It simply means that any instance or volume (resource) created to support your application function should be able to be recreated in some sort of automated fashion. Instilling the *pets versus cattle* analogy. It is no longer the days of attempting to bring a sick VM back to life; the need of the hour is to destroy the instance, recreate it and off you go again. These principles remove the want for instance backups. With that said, there will be cases when you may want to have a backup of an instance. So, let's first examine the capability of taking an instance backup.

The OpenStack compute service (Nova) functionality of backing up an instance behaves just as any traditional backup process. The purpose of taking a backup of an instance is to preserve the current state of the instances for possible recovery later. Just as in any other back process, you can determine the type of backup and rotation schedule. Some possible backup type parameters can be *daily* or *weekly*. The rotation schedule will represent the number of backups to keep. A working example of the instance backup command via the Nova CLI is as follows:

```
$ nova backup <instance> <backup name> <backup-type> <rotation>
```

```
$ nova backup testinst bck-testinst weekly 5
```

In full transparency, the Nova backup functionality is not in a fully operational state, as of the time the book was written. The backup command at this point in time is just a hook put into Nova to set up for future OpenStack service(s) focused solely on data protection. The OpenStack Data Protection service, code name **Raksha**, will be responsible for helping automate data protection tasks, such as backups. Raksha is still under development and will appear in the upcoming OpenStack release. You can read more about Raksha here https://wiki.openstack.org/wiki/Raksha.

Now we can move on to snapshots. The Nova functionality of taking a snapshot of an instance is similar to a backup, but instead of keeping the backup for recovery purposes it is stored by the image service (glance) as an image template. That image template can then be used to create additional instances similar to the instance the original snapshot was taken from. It is like making a rubber stamp copy of the instance.

Note that taking a traditional snapshot of an instance will temporarily pause the instance until the process is complete. If you want to take a snapshot without pausing the instance, please review the *Live Snapshots* capability details found at http://docs.openstack.org/openstack-ops/content/snapshots.html.

I often liken the snapshot process to making a *golden* or *gold* image of a server that will be used to build additional servers. The steps taken will be exactly the same. You will create the instance with the required OS, install necessary software packages, make suggested OS and application security tweaks, certify the applications functionality and then create the snapshot. Having the snapshot capability at your fingertips without needing any third-party software is indeed yet another powerful tool that OpenStack offers.

A working example of the instance snapshot command via the Nova CLI is as follows:

```
$ nova image-create <instance> <snapshot name>
```

```
$ nova image-create testinst snp-testinst
```

Hopefully, this will help you to provide clear definitions around the differences between instance backups and snapshots. Let us now examine the steps required to manually create them using the CLI.

 For simplicity purposes, we will demonstrate the manual commands using the OpenStack CLI only.

Creating backups and snapshots manually

As stated earlier, the compute service (Nova) handles the task of creating instance backups and snapshots. Similar to every OpenStack service, you must authenticate either by sourcing the OpenRC file discussed in the *Chapter 1, An Introduction to OpenStack*, or by passing the authentication parameters in line with the command. The two tasks individually require different parameter values to be provided in order to successfully execute the command, as shown in the following examples.

Instance backup using OpenRC file:

```
$ source openrc
$ nova backup <instance> <backup name> <backup-type> <rotation>
```

Instance backup passing authentication parameters in line:

```
$ nova --os-username=<OS_USERNAME> --os-password=<OS_PASSWORD>  --os-
tenant-name=<OS_TENANT_NAME> --os-auth-url=<OS_AUTH_URL> backup
<instance> <backup name> <backup-type> <rotation>
```

Once the command is executed, no output is written back on the screen. You can then execute the `glance image-list` command to confirm the update.

A real-life working example with an OpenRC file will look similar to this:

```
$ source openrc
$ nova list
$ nova backup test-058507b2-8a5d-47e5-9bc6-690b71838f5e bck-test-
058507b2-8a5d-47e5-9bc6-690b71838f5e weekly 3
```

The output of the `glance image-list` command will then be:

With the preceding command, you can supply the instance ID or name. The example shown uses the instance name. After sourcing the OpenRC file, the `nova list` command is executed in order to take note of the instance ID or name that you wish to back up. The `nova backup` command can then be executed once you have that information.

> The image service, code name **Glance**, is responsible for maintaining the inventory of backups, snapshots and any images manually uploaded by the cloud operator. To view the available inventory, you will have to issue Glance CLI commands and/or view them via the **Horizon** dashboard under the **Images** tab.

Instance snapshot using the OpenRC file is as follows:

```
$ source openrc
$ nova image-create <instance> <snapshot name>
```

Instance snapshot passing the authentication parameters in line is as follows:

```
$ nova --os-username=<OS_USERNAME> --os-password=<OS_PASSWORD>  --os-
tenant-name=<OS_TENANT_NAME> --os-auth-url=<OS_AUTH_URL> image-create
<instance> <image name>
```

Once the command is executed, no output is written back on the screen. You can then execute the `glance image-list` command to confirm the update.

A real-life working example with an OpenRC file will look similar to this:

```
$ source openrc
$ nova list
$ nova image-create test-058507b2-8a5d-47e5-9bc6-690b71838f5e snp-test-
058507b2-8a5d-47e5-9bc6-690b71838f5e
```

The output of the `glance image-list` command will then be:

Now that we have covered how to create the instance backups and snapshots, it feels only right to demonstrate how you can use them. Particularly, I will focus on utilizing the instance backups since I have noticed a severe lack of documentation around this functionality.

Restore an instance backup

Although the instance backup functionality is not 100 percent active from the perspective of a scheduled job/automation, you can still use instance backups to restore an instance back to a particular point in time. In order to do this, you will have to use the `nova rebuild` command within the Nova CLI. This command will signal the instance to shutdown, re-image the instance using the backup file referenced and then reboot the instance.

A working example of the Nova rebuild command via the Nova CLI is as follows:

```
$ nova rebuild <instance> <image name>


$ nova rebuild test-058507b2-8a5d-47e5-9bc6-690b71838f5e bck-test-
058507b2-8a5d-47e5-9bc6-690b71838f5e
```

The Nova rebuild command has quite a few optional arguments that can be passed with the command. Those optional arguments can do things, such as reset the admin password or change the name of the instance, for example. I suggest taking a look at the OpenStack CLI documentation, which can be found at `http://docs.openstack.org/cli-reference/content/novaclient_commands.html#novaclient_subcommand_rebuild`.

Automation considerations

Automating this task was pretty straightforward and did not require any new framework decisions. All the other automation decisions we reviewed previously were carried over.

There is one area worth highlighting that you may also face when automating OpenStack tasks using the CLI. The default output of the CLI is *pretty-printed* (using the Python `prettytable` module), which at times is not so pretty when you want to sort through the output. Some CLI commands give the option of specific formatting, but in the event the command does not allow it, you have other options. This is where again the `awk` command becomes your very close ally. You will note that in the next section the specific use of the `awk` command is to filter out the values that we need for the next task within the role.

It feels like we are ready to proceed with creating our next playbook and role.

Coding the playbook and roles

The playbook and role that we will now create will allow you to take a snapshot of all instances within a single tenant at one time. This distinct task was chosen to try to keep the role simple and not to overcomplicate the tasks. You can also create a role to snapshot or backup all the instances in all the tenants with the removal of just one parameter. Pretty awesome right? Well, send your thank you cards to Ansible for that.

At the beginning of the chapter, we reviewed the process of how to take instance backups and snapshots. It was a very simple two-step process. For the purpose of automating this task, we have to add an additional step to the process. That step will be to get the tenant ID for the tenant we plan to take the snapshot(s) from. So in the big picture, the steps will be. Step 1 is to record the tenant ID in which you wish to take instance snapshot(s) for. Step 2 is to list all the instance IDs from the tenant. Then finally, step 3 is to actually take the instance snapshot(s).

Since we are only creating a role in this example, we can start by the `main.yml` file within the role directory named `create-snapshot/tasks`. The beginning contents of this file will look similar to this:

```
---

- name: Retrieve tenantID
shell: keystone --os-username={{ OS_USERNAME }} --os-password={{ OS_
PASSWORD }} --os-tenant-name={{ OS_TENANT_NAME }} --os-auth-url={{
OS_AUTH_URL }}
tenant-list | awk '/ {{ tenantname }} / { print $2 }'
register: tenantid
```

The first step of pulling the tenant ID is straightforward with the use of the `awk` command and pipe (|) symbol. This approach is something you will see in a lot of the OpenStack documentation. It allows you to take the output of one command and filter out the parts you want to keep. First, we will execute the `tenant-list` command, and that output will then be used with a filter, the filter will search for the tenant name provided via the variable named `tenantname`, and finally, it will output the second column value from the original `tenant-list` command. That final output will then be registered with the variable named `tenantid`. The `tenantname` variable is defined the same way as shown in the last chapter.

Remember the `shell` module is used here because we are executing the commands that require operations specific to shell.

The next task will now list out all the instance IDs from the tenant. The code to accomplish this looks similar to the following:

```
- name: Retrieve instance id from tenant
shell: nova --os-username={{ OS_USERNAME }} --os-password={{ OS_
PASSWORD }} --os-tenant-name={{ OS_TENANT_NAME }} --os-auth-url={{
OS_AUTH_URL }}
list --all-tenants --tenant {{ tenantid.stdout }} --minimal | awk 'NR
> 3 { print $2 }'
register: instid
```

This task is very similar to the first one, except that we are using the Nova CLI instead to list the instances and filter out just the IDs; thus, removing all leading or trailing characters. I found that the `nova image-create` command when using Ansible was very specific about how the instance ID/name had to be provided. In order to accomplish this, I decided to use one of the `awk` command built-in variables called NR. The NR variable (number of records) within `awk` is intended to supply you with the number of records or the line number of the content being filtered. In turn, the NR variable can be used to focus the examination on certain lines. Here we use a variable to skip the first three lines of the CLI output. The following example shows what the normal output will be:

```
root@infra1_utility_container-c750da76:~# nova list --all-tenants --minimal
+--------------------------------------+--------------------------------------+
| ID                                   | Name                                 |
+--------------------------------------+--------------------------------------+
| 058507b2-8a5d-47e5-9bc6-690b71838f5e | test-058507b2-8a5d-47e5-9bc6-690b71838f5e |
| 1ae02fae-93ca-4485-a797-e7f781a7a25b | test-1ae02fae-93ca-4485-a797-e7f781a7a25b |
| 2549262c-5322-4fdc-b5e7-4c1da7af3f7f | test-2549262c-5322-4fdc-b5e7-4c1da7af3f7f |
| 5276e847-bbb2-4650-9240-66d178494703 | testB-5276e847-bbb2-4650-9240-66d178494703 |
| b814c1c0-c151-40ee-928b-cfd7d599710f | testB-b814c1c0-c151-40ee-928b-cfd7d599710f |
+--------------------------------------+--------------------------------------+
```

Now, add the following command:

```
awk 'NR > 3 { print $2 }'
```

When `awk` command is added the output looks as follows:

```
root@infra1_utility_container-c750da76:~# nova list --all-tenants --minimal | awk 'NR > 3 { print $2 }'
058507b2-8a5d-47e5-9bc6-690b71838f5e
1ae02fae-93ca-4485-a797-e7f781a7a25b
2549262c-5322-4fdc-b5e7-4c1da7af3f7f
5276e847-bbb2-4650-9240-66d178494703
b814c1c0-c151-40ee-928b-cfd7d599710f
```

Finally, now that we have our list of instances we can conclude with the last task of taking the snapshot(s). The code to do this will look like the following example:

```
- name: Create instance snapshot
  command: nova --os-username={{ OS_USERNAME }} --os-password={{ OS_PASSWORD }} --os-tenant-name={{ OS_TENANT_NAME }} --os-auth-url={{ OS_AUTH_URL }}
  image-create {{ item }} {{ tenantname }}-snap-{{ item }}
  with_items: instid.stdout_lines
```

Just as in the previous chapter, defining the {{item}} parameter value with the module allows us to loop through multiple packages listed inside the with_items statement. Also, remember that getting the output after registering the values into a variable within Ansible requires you to query the stdout or stdout_lines section of the JSON data structure. We then re-purposed the tenant name and instance ID to name the snapshot for easy future reference. The snapshot name itself can be anything you desire, I just felt this naming convention made the most sense.

When the role is executed no output is generated in this particular case. If you want to provide an output to confirm the successful execution of the task, you can add the glance image-list command as an additional task in your role and either have the task output printed to the screen or saved in a file. An example of printing the output to the screen will look similar to the following example:

```
- name: Confirm instance snapshot(s)
  shell: glance --os-username={{ OS_USERNAME }} --os-password={{ OS_
PASSWORD }} --os-tenant-name={{ OS_TENANT_NAME }} --os-auth-url={{
OS_AUTH_URL }}
image-list | awk 'NR > 3 { print $4 }'
  register: snapchk

- name: Image list output
  debug: msg="{{ item }}"
  with_items: snapchk.stdout_lines
```

You have now completed your third OpenStack administration role. To support this role, we now need to create the variable file that will go along with it. The variable file will be named main.yml, and located in the create-snapshot/vars directory.

 Note that the values defined in the variable file are intended to be changed before each execution for normal everyday use.

For this role, there was only one variable that was needed:

```
---
tenantname: MRKT-Proj01
```

This variable is intended to be a single value of one of the tenant names for which the instance snapshot(s) will be taken.

Now that our variable file is created, we can move on to creating the master playbook file. The file will be named snapshot-tenant.yml and saved to the root of the playbook directory.

The playbook and role names can be anything you choose. Specific names have been provided here in order to enable you to easily follow along and reference the completed code found in the GitHub repository. The only warning is whatever you decide to name the roles must remain uniform when referenced from within the playbook(s).

The contents of the `snapshot-tenant.yml` file will be:

```
---
# This playbook used to demo OpenStack Juno quota updates.

- hosts: util_container
user: root
remote_user: root
sudo: yes
roles:
create-snapshot
```

The summary of this file will be as follows:

```
hosts          # the host or host group to execute the playbook against

user           # the user to use when executing the playbook locally

remote_user    # the user to use when executing the playbook on the
remote host(s)

sudo           # will tell Ansible to sudo into the above user on the
remote host(s)

roles          # provide a list of roles to execute as part of this
playbook
```

All that is left is to populate our host inventory file and the global variable file. Since we already created these in the last chapter, there is no need to repeat this process. The values defined earlier will remain the same. The following is a quick recap of how those files are configured.

The `hosts` file in the root of the `playbook` directory:

```
[localhost]
localhost ansible_connection=local

[util_container]
172.29.236.199
```

The global variable file inside the `group_vars/` directory is as follows:

```
# Here are variables related globally to the util_container host group

OS_USERNAME: ansible
OS_PASSWORD: passwd
OS_TENANT_NAME: admin
OS_AUTH_URL: http://172.29.236.7:35357/v2.0
```

Word of caution

Due to the contents of this file, it should be stored as a secure file within whatever code repository you may use to store your Ansible playbooks/ roles. Gaining access to this information could compromise your OpenStack cloud security.

Great job in completing your third administration playbook and role! As always, we will finish up the chapter with a quick review of the playbook and role just created.

Playbook and role review

Let's jump right into examining the role we created called `create-snapshot`. The completed role and file named `main.yml` located in the `create-snapshot/tasks` directory looks similar to this:

```
---

- name: Retrieve tenantID
shell: keystone --os-username={{ OS_USERNAME }} --os-password={{ OS_
PASSWORD }} --os-tenant-name={{ OS_TENANT_NAME }} --os-auth-url={{
OS_AUTH_URL }}
tenant-list | awk '/ {{ tenantname }} / { print $2 }'
register: tenantid

- name: Retrieve instance id from tenant
shell: nova --os-username={{ OS_USERNAME }} --os-password={{ OS_
PASSWORD }} --os-tenant-name={{ OS_TENANT_NAME }} --os-auth-url={{
OS_AUTH_URL }}
list --all-tenants --tenant {{ tenantid.stdout }} --minimal | awk 'NR
> 3 { print $2 }'
register: instid
```

```
- name: Create instance snapshot
command: nova --os-username={{ OS_USERNAME }} --os-password={{ OS_
PASSWORD }} --os-tenant-name={{ OS_TENANT_NAME }} --os-auth-url={{
OS_AUTH_URL }}
image-create {{ item }} {{ tenantname }}-snap-{{ item }}
with_items: instid.stdout_lines
```

The corresponding variable file named `main.yml`, located in the `create-snapshot/vars` directory, for this role will look similar to this:

```
---

tenantname: MRKT-Proj01
```

Next, the master playbook file named `snapshot-tenant.yml`, located in the root of the `playbook` directory, will look similar to this:

```
---

# This playbook used to demo OpenStack Juno quota updates.

- hosts: util_container
user: root
remote_user: root
sudo: yes
roles:
create-snapshot
```

Following this we created the `hosts` file, which is also located in the root of the `playbook` directory.

```
[localhost]
localhost ansible_connection=local

[util_container]
172.29.236.199
```

Finally, creating the global variable file named `util_container` and saving it to the `group_vars/` directory of the playbook will complete the playbook.

```
# Here are variables related globally to the util_container host group

OS_USERNAME: ansible
OS_PASSWORD: passwd
OS_TENANT_NAME: admin
OS_AUTH_URL: http://172.29.236.7:35357/v2.0
```

The complete set of codes can again be found in the following GitHub repository: `https://github.com/os-admin-with-ansible/os-admin-with-ansible`.

We cannot finish up this chapter without first testing out our work. Assuming that you have cloned the GitHub repository, the command to test out the playbook from the deployment node will be as follows:

```
$ cd os-admin-with-ansible
$ ansible-playbook -i hosts snapshot-tenant.yml
```

Summary

Once you get started with creating playbooks and roles with Ansible, you will find that you are able to reuse a lot of code for many different purposes. In this chapter, we were able to create another role very similar to the last chapter but include a totally different task very quickly and easily. Always remember to design your roles to be the base generic task, as much as possible. I sincerely cannot emphasize that tip enough. It can be the difference between taking minutes/hours or days to automate something.

Some of the things we covered in this chapter are: we defined and described the difference between instance backups and snapshots, explained the process of how to manually create backups and snapshots using the OpenStack CLI, reviewed an example of how to utilize an instance backup, and then finally developed the Ansible playbook and role to automate creating snapshot(s) of all instances within a specified tenant. I am very excited to move on to the next chapter, where we will examine the process of migrating instances between compute nodes. This is surely an administration task you will face while managing your OpenStack cloud. It is rather a controversial topic as well because many do not either know that this functionality exists within OpenStack or do not believe that this function works well. In the next chapter, we will try to clear up the unwarranted confusion by demonstrating how to migrate the instance(s) manually and then take it a step further by automating it. For those of us who are cloud operators, the next chapter will be worth its value in gold. You do not want to skip the next chapter; it will certainly be worth it. *Chapter 6, Migrating Instances*, here we come!

6
Migrating Instances

In this chapter, we will cover the task of migrating instances using the native OpenStack capability built into the Compute service (Nova). As mentioned earlier, the existence of this functionality is unknown by many. Before this chapter is over, we will prove this capability by demonstrating how to manually migrate instances; as well as, review the steps required to automate this task and finally create a playbook with roles to fully automate instance migration to a specified compute node.

In this chapter, we will cover the following topics,

- Instance migration
- Automation considerations
- Coding the playbook and roles
- Playbook and role review

Instance migration

Whenever the topic of instance migration comes up, it normally ends in a spirited conversation among my OpenStack peers for various reasons. So as a responsible adult, I will go on record and say instance migration is not perfect.

It has its flaws and can be quirky at best. Migration, whether live or not, has a practical use case in your OpenStack cloud. Within OpenStack, you have the capability of migrating instances from one compute node to another. You may do this for maintenance purposes and/or to rebalance the resource utilization across the cloud. Also, keep in mind that there are multiple ways to clear out a compute node for maintenance and we will cover this in more detail in *Chapter 8, Deploying OpenStack Features*.

As mentioned earlier, the OpenStack Compute service (Nova) has the functionality to migrate instances in a traditional method and the ability to live-migrate an instance as well.

We will first examine the traditional migration method and its properties.

The traditional migration method moves an instance by shutting down the instance, copying the instance image or file to the next available compute node, starting the instance on the new node, and lastly removing the instance from the original node. The areas to focus on in this method are:

- The instance is shutdown

- The instance image or file will take time to copy to a new compute node

- The new compute node selection is done by Nova Scheduler, you can not assign one without the additional steps required

- The instance is then brought back online once the copy is completed

Note that some may consider this method to be intrusive. The idea of shutting down an instance to move it was not a desirable scenario back in the virtualization days. Remember that we are in a new era, *the era of cloud and disposable resources*.

Since resources are readily available and you have the control to determine how to consume these resources, there should be no issue in taking an instance offline. Right? Yes, I know it will take a while to shake that *pet* mentality, you will get there. In the event the circumstances allow for this, which normally means you did a good job distributing across your hypervisors the instances running your application(s), you can very easily use this method to migrate instances.

A working example of the traditional instance migration command via the Nova CLI will be as follows:

```
$ nova migrate <instance>
$ nova migrate testinst
```

The other migration method would be to perform live instance migration. This method will remove the requirement of shutting down the instance, as it was highlighted in the traditional migration process described above. Instead of shutting down the instance, it is suspended (still in a running state) till it is reassigned to a new compute node. There are additional system requirements that are needed in order to leverage the live-migration functionality. The requirements are as follows:

- Some sort of shared or external storage capability must exist between your compute nodes

- With live-migration, you can select the new compute node but you must assure that the new node has the resources required for the new instance
- The old and new compute nodes must have the same CPU (OpenStack releases before Kilo may encounter an issue if this is not the case)

The first requirement is the most important one on the list and deserves some further explanation. The additional storage requirement can be covered in three different ways:

- The first way to satisfy the demand is to configure your hypervisors to store and have access to the shared storage; for instance, placement. It means that the instances are stored on the shared storage device and not on the ephemeral storage. This could involve mounting NFS share on the compute node to be used to store instances or through fiber channel sharing a LUN across the compute nodes, for example.
- The second approach to satisfy the shared or external storage requirement can be to leverage direct block storage, where your instances are backed by image-based root disks.
- The third and final approach could be the boot from volume storage capability. This is where you are booting instances off of Cinder-based volumes. Of course, you will need the block storage service (Cinder) enabled and configured within your OpenStack cloud.

The key message, in relation to utilizing the live-migration capability, within Nova is that your *instances must exist on some sort of shared or external storage and cannot use ephemeral storage local to the compute node.*

A working example of an instance live-migration command via the Nova CLI would be as follows:

```
$ nova live-migration <instance><new compute node>
$ nova live-migration testinst compute01
```

As mentioned earlier, the whole concept of instance migration can range from being very simple all the way to being extremely complex. We hope that you can now clearly understand what is required and the process followed during an instance migration. Let's now examine the process of manually migrating an instance using the CLI.

For simplicity purposes, we will demonstrate the manual commands using the OpenStack CLI only.

Manually migrating instances

The Compute service (Nova) is responsible for managing the instance migration process. Nova behind the scenes will execute all the steps needed to reassign the instance(s) to the new node and the movement of the instance image or file. Similar to every OpenStack service, you must authenticate against Keystone either by sourcing the OpenRC file discussed in *Chapter 1, An Introduction to OpenStack*, or by passing authentication parameters in-line with the command. The two tasks, individually, require different parameter values to be provided in order to successfully execute the command. See the following example:

For instance migration using OpenRC file, use the following commands:

```
$ source openrc
$ nova migrate <instance>
```

For instance backup passing the authentication parameters inline:

```
$ nova --os-username=<OS_USERNAME> --os-password=<OS_PASSWORD>  --os-tenant-name=<OS_TENANT_NAME> --os-auth-url=<OS_AUTH_URL> migrate
<instance>
```

With the `nova migrate` command you can add an optional additional argument to the command to report the instance migration process. The `--poll` argument can be used with various other Nova commands as well. It is something I will not use regularly when automating OpenStack tasks, for obvious reasons. Since the migration process can take some time and we are executing the task manually, it helps to keep track of its progress. An example of adding that optional argument would be:

```
$ nova migrate --poll <instance>
```

Since the traditional `nova migrate` command without the `--poll` argument does not output anything on the screen, you will need to execute a subsequent command to check on the migration status. The follow-up command will be the `nova migration-list` command.

A real life working example with an OpenRC file will look something similar to this:

```
$ source openrc
$ nova list
$ nova migrate test-1ae02fae-93ca-4485-a797-e7f781a7a25b
```

The output of the `nova migration-list` command will appear similar to:

The complete output provided in the preceding command will vary, based on any previous migrations executed. The key information to focus on is the `Status` of the migration for the instance you just attempted to migrate. The status will be reported as either *migrating* or *finished*. Once the status is updated to *finished*, you can confirm the migration of the instance. After migration the instance will be in a `VERIFY_RESIZE` state by default, whether or not if you actually resized it. If you issue a `nova show` command the output will appear similar to this:

You will then need to execute the `nova resize-confirm` command to put the instance back in the `ACTIVE` state. The following example demonstrates this task:

```
$ nova resize-confirm test-1ae02fae-93ca-4485-a797-e7f781a7a25b
```

At this point you are good to go! Your instance will get migrated to a new compute node and run in an active state. For those of us who have learned to accept the traditional migration process, the next statement normally is, *"Why can't I migrate an instance to a specific compute node, using the nova migrate command?"*. We will talk about this in the next section.

Migrating an instance to a specific compute node

The honest and straight answer to the above question is, I have no clue why this capability was not included. The good thing, just like most things within OpenStack, is that there is always a way to get it to do what you want.

 Note that the steps outlined in the next section are 100% a workaround (a mid-grade dirty workaround) and *should not* be used within a production environment, without first executing multiple levels of testing to ensure the expected functionality.

As covered in the preceding sections, you cannot migrate an instance to a specific compute node using the traditional migration method. The option just does not exist (hope that changes soon). However, you can trick the Nova scheduler to place the instance on a selected compute node by disabling the other compute nodes. The Nova scheduler will then have no choice but to migrate the instance to the compute node you selected. Yes, in your mind you just called me an idiot; don't worry, it is not as intrusive as it sounds on paper.

The OpenStack control plane services are designed to report the status of the distributed components, such as compute nodes and/or cinder nodes; for example, the report received is stored within the OpenStack database and this is how the control plane services know if a particular node is up or down. Similarly, the control plane services can also force a report of a nodes status.

The Compute service (Nova) is an example service that can force a report on the status of a compute node. This will simply mark a compute node as up or down within the database and never actually *do* anything physically to the compute node. All the instances running on those compute nodes will remain running and the overall functionality of the node will go unchanged. However, the time for which the node is disabled within the database will prevent new instances to be created there. If you have a very busy and continuously changing OpenStack cloud and are not using a segregated set of compute nodes, this work-around is probably not a wise idea.

Due to its intrusive nature, it feels like a perfect administrative task to try and automate. With something like this, timing and accuracy is very critical. Wasting something as small as a minute could equate to the failure of being able to create any number of new instances by the cloud consumers inside your OpenStack cloud. For tasks of this nature, automation is king. In the next few sections, we will review the required steps to automate this task.

Automation considerations

This task also did not require any new framework decisions. All the other automation decisions we reviewed previously and carried over.

Before we start, it is worth noting that when automating a task, such as this one, (migrating an instance and disabling compute nodes) it is best to collect the details concerning them both before and after the migration. Having those details will simplify the process of reversing your changes, if required. Yes, this will add additional tasks to your role making it slightly more complex but still well worth it.

With that said, we are now ready to proceed to create our next playbook and role.

Coding the playbook and roles

In this section, we will now create the playbook and role that will allow you to migrate an instance to a specific compute node using the traditional `nova migrate` command. Unlike the other tasks that we have created so far, there is really only one way to handle this task. We will take the steps outlined in the preceding two sections, automate them to make sure that we have to supply only a few variable values, and then execute only one command.

This chapter started off with talking about instance migration and how there are two options within Nova to handle this; namely, traditional migration and live-migration. The traditional migration process is basically a one step process but in order to properly automate this task we will need to add a few more steps to the process. A brief outline of the tasks that we will have to create are:

1. List the compute nodes.
2. Collect pre-migration instance details.
3. Disable all compute nodes except for the one we want the instance to migrate to.
4. Migrate the instance.

5. Enable all compute nodes.

6. Confirm instance migration.

7. Collect post-migration instance details.

Since we are only creating a role in this example, we can start with the `main.yml` file within the role directory named `instance-migrate/tasks`. The initial contents of this file will look similar to the following code:

```
---

- name: Retrieve hypervisor list
  shell: nova --os-username={{ OS_USERNAME }} --os-password={{ OS_
PASSWORD }} --os-tenant-name={{ OS_TENANT_NAME }} --os-auth-url={{
OS_AUTH_URL }}
  hypervisor-list | awk 'NR > 3' | awk '$4 != "{{ desthype }}" { print
$4 }'
  register: hypelist
```

The first step to retrieving the complete list of compute nodes within your OpenStack cloud is very easy if we use the `nova hypervisor-list` command. Once you get these results, it is best to strip down the output to provide just the information you need. Again, we will do this using the `awk` command and pipe (|) symbol. You will note that this is similar to how we did it in the last chapter. Remember that the `shell` module is used here because we are executing commands that require shell-specific operations.

For this particular task, we have to get a bit magical with the `awk` commands:

```
awk 'NR > 3' | awk '$4 != "{{ desthype }}" { print $4 }'
```

Not only will it pull off the first three lines of the standard CLI output, it will also check the fourth column and print the complete output excluding the value within the `{{ desthype }}` variable being passed. The consolidated output will then be registered into a variable named `hypelist`.

The next task will now collect the pre-migration instance details that will be stored for later use within the role. The code to accomplish this looks similar to the following code:

```
- name: Collect pre-migration instance details
  shell: nova --os-username={{ OS_USERNAME }} --os-password={{ OS_
PASSWORD }} --os-tenant-name={{ OS_TENANT_NAME }} --os-auth-url={{
OS_AUTH_URL }}
  list --name {{ instance }} --fields OS-EXT-SRV-ATTR:host | awk 'NR >
3' | awk '{ print $4 }'
  register: preinststat
```

For this task, we are again using the Nova CLI to provide the instance details using the `nova list` command. You could have, just as well, used the `nova show` command to list the instance details. A distinct difference between the two commands is that with the `nova list` command you can choose which fields to return for the output. To do this, add the optional argument of `--fields` and a comma-delimited list of instance related field names to the command.

The following example will return only the instance ID, name, and status:

```
nova list --fields name,status
```

In our particular case, we want to know the compute node that the particular instance is currently running on. Thus our command will look similar to:

```
nova list --name {{ instance }} --fields OS-EXT-SRV-ATTR:host
```

The output will look similar to the following screenshot:

```
root@infra1_utility_container-762f6a29:~# nova list --name test6-03dd766b-04e4-4eff-83a8-a7e47f90c516 --fields OS-EXT-SR\
+--------------------------------------+------------------------+
| ID                                   | OS-EXT-SRV-ATTR: Host  |
+--------------------------------------+------------------------+
| 03dd766b-04e4-4eff-83a8-a7e47f90c516 | 021579-compute01       |
+--------------------------------------+------------------------+
```

The third task will be to disable the compute node(s) that you do not want the instance to migrate to; remember that we are only disabling the compute nodes within Nova and not physically changing the state of the compute node(s). The code to do this will look similar to the following example:

```
- name: Disable unselected hypervisors
  command: nova --os-username={{ OS_USERNAME }} --os-password={{ OS_
  PASSWORD }} --os-tenant-name={{ OS_TENANT_NAME }} --os-auth-url={{
  OS_AUTH_URL }}
  service-disable {{ item }} nova-compute --reason '{{ migreason }}'
  with_items: hypelist.stdout_lines
```

With use of the `nova service-disable` command, you can tell Nova to disable any particular Nova related service on remote hosts. In order to have Nova scheduler ignore or skip a compute node, you need to disable the *nova-compute* service. The command also requires a reason to be provided, of which will be stored in the Nova database for later reference if required. It is in this task where we will use the list of compute node(s) stored in the `hypelist` variable collected earlier.

Note that we will not disable the compute node that we want the instance to be migrated to, as we have filtered it out of the list already.

Moving onto the fourth task, we will now execute the instance migration. At this point, only the compute node you specify is enabled and nothing special needs to be done in reference to the `nova migrate` command except adding the `--poll` argument, so we can pause the role execution until the migration completes. See the following supporting code:

```
- name: Migrate instance
command: nova --os-username={{ OS_USERNAME }} --os-password={{ OS_
PASSWORD }} --os-tenant-name={{ OS_TENANT_NAME }} --os-auth-url={{
OS_AUTH_URL }}
migrate --poll {{ instance }}
```

Once the migration is completed, we need to immediately enable the compute node(s) that were disabled. One of the things I appreciate about OpenStack is, if you are given a command to disable something, you are normally given a command to re-enable it. So, we will simply execute the `nova service-enable` command and we will use the `hypelist` variable to provide the list of compute node(s) to execute against. The following code is used:

```
- name: Enable the disabled hypervisors
command: nova --os-username={{ OS_USERNAME }} --os-password={{ OS_
PASSWORD }} --os-tenant-name={{ OS_TENANT_NAME }} --os-auth-url={{
OS_AUTH_URL }}
service-enable {{ item }} nova-compute
with_items: hypelist.stdout_lines
```

Now that the migration is complete and the compute node(s) is enabled, we can focus on completing the instance migration process. The last step in an instance migration process is to notify Nova that you acknowledge that the instance was moved. At first glance, I could live without this step, but in hindsight some sort of confirmation does make overall sense. The code for this task is as follows:

```
- name: Confirm instance migration
command: nova --os-username={{ OS_USERNAME }} --os-password={{ OS_
PASSWORD }} --os-tenant-name={{ OS_TENANT_NAME }} --os-auth-url={{
OS_AUTH_URL }}
resize-confirm {{ instance }}
```

The last two final tasks will be used to provide the individual running the playbook with a visual confirmation of what was done. You can consider this more of an automation fail safe and less of a requirement. With an administrative task as complex as this, it is always a good common practice to output some details of what was changed on your system:

```
- name: Collect post-migration instance details
  shell: nova --os-username={{ OS_USERNAME }} --os-password={{ OS_
PASSWORD }} --os-tenant-name={{ OS_TENANT_NAME }} --os-auth-url={{
OS_AUTH_URL }}
  list --name {{ instance }} --fields OS-EXT-SRV-ATTR:host,status | awk
'NR > 3' | awk '{ print $4 " and has a status of " $6 }' | awk 'NR ==
1'
  register: postinststat

- name: Show instance location and status
  debug: msg="{{ instance }} was migrated from {{ item.0 }} to {{ item.1
}}"
  with_together:
  - preinststat.stdout_lines
  - postinststat.stdout_lines
```

These two tasks will first collect post-migration instance details and then use the information collected from the `preinststat` and `postinststat` variables to output to the screen a synopsis of the changes. The synopsis template used will be:

```
<instance migrated> was migrated from <compute node> to <compute node>
and has a status of <instance current status>
```

 Feel free to go in and change it to fit your needs. This is just my opinionated approach. It felt right to keep it simple, while still supplying the pertinent details we care about when handling a migration. Upon the review of the playbook recap, if something went wrong and/or was implemented incorrectly, you should be able to quickly target steps for remediation.

Congratulations again; you have just completed your fourth OpenStack administration role. To support this role, we now need to create the variable file that will go along with it—the variable file named `main.yml`, which will be located in the `instance-migrate/vars` directory.

 Keep in mind that the values defined in the variable file are intended to be changed before each execution, for normal everyday use.

For this role, we kept it pretty simple on the variables front and only needed to define three variables:

```
---
desthype: 021579-compute02
instance: testG-2c00131c-c2c7-4eae-aa90-981e54ca7b04
migreason: "Migrating instance to new compute node"
```

Let's take a moment to break down each variable. The summary will be:

```
desthype    # this value would be the name of the compute node you wish
to migrate the instance to

instance    # the name of the instance to be migrated

migreason: # a string encapsulated in quotes to explain the reason for
migrating the instance (keep the string brief)
```

With the variable file completed, we can now move on to creating the master playbook file. The file will be named `migrate.yml` and saved to the root of the playbook directory.

> The playbook and role names can be anything you choose. The specific names have been provided here in order to allow for you to easily follow along and reference the completed code found in the GitHub repository. The only warning is, whatever you decide to name the roles must remain uniform when referenced from within the playbook(s).

The contents of the `migrate.yml` file will be:

```
---
# This playbook used to migrate instance to specific compute node.

- hosts: util_container
user: root
remote_user: root
sudo: yes
roles:
- instance-migrate
```

The summary of this file is as follows:

```
hosts         # the host or host group to execute the playbook against

user          # the user to use when executing the playbook locally

remote_user   # the user to use when executing the playbook on the
remote host(s)

sudo          # will tell Ansible to sudo into the above user on the
remote host(s)

roles         # provide a list of roles to execute as part of this
playbook
```

Adding content to our host inventory file and the global variable file was done two chapters ago, so we already have that part covered. The values defined earlier will remain the same. The following is a quick recap of how those files are configured.

The hosts file in the root of the playbook directory:

```
[localhost]
localhostansible_connection=local

[util_container]
172.29.236.199
```

The global variable file inside the group_vars/ directory:

```
# Here are variables related globally to the util_container host group

OS_USERNAME: ansible
OS_PASSWORD: passwd
OS_TENANT_NAME: admin
OS_AUTH_URL: http://172.29.236.7:35357/v2.0
```

A word of caution

Due to the contents of this file, it should be stored as a secure file within whatever code repository you may want to use to store your Ansible playbooks/roles. Gaining access to this information can compromise your OpenStack cloud security.

We are moving along very smoothly now, smile, you did it! Hoping that by this point everything is becoming a bit clearer. Keeping with our tradition, we will finish up the chapter with a quick review of the playbook and the role just created.

Playbook and role review

Let's jump right into examining the role we created called `instance-migrate`. The completed role and file named `main.yml` located in the `instance-migrate/tasks` directory looks similar to the following example:

```
---

- name: Retrieve hypervisor list
shell: nova --os-username={{ OS_USERNAME }} --os-password={{ OS_
PASSWORD }} --os-tenant-name={{ OS_TENANT_NAME }} --os-auth-url={{
OS_AUTH_URL }}
hypervisor-list | awk 'NR > 3' | awk '$4 != "{{ desthype }}" { print
$4 }'
register: hypelist

- name: Collect pre-migration instance details
shell: nova --os-username={{ OS_USERNAME }} --os-password={{ OS_
PASSWORD }} --os-tenant-name={{ OS_TENANT_NAME }} --os-auth-url={{
OS_AUTH_URL }}
list --name {{ instance }} --fields OS-EXT-SRV-ATTR:host | awk 'NR >
3' | awk '{ print $4 }'
register: preinststat

- name: Disable unselected hypervisors
command: nova --os-username={{ OS_USERNAME }} --os-password={{ OS_
PASSWORD }} --os-tenant-name={{ OS_TENANT_NAME }} --os-auth-url={{
OS_AUTH_URL }}
service-disable {{ item }} nova-compute --reason '{{ migreason }}'
with_items: hypelist.stdout_lines

- name: Migrate instance
command: nova --os-username={{ OS_USERNAME }} --os-password={{ OS_
PASSWORD }} --os-tenant-name={{ OS_TENANT_NAME }} --os-auth-url={{
OS_AUTH_URL }}
migrate --poll {{ instance }}

- name: Enable the disabled hypervisors
command: nova --os-username={{ OS_USERNAME }} --os-password={{ OS_
PASSWORD }} --os-tenant-name={{ OS_TENANT_NAME }} --os-auth-url={{
OS_AUTH_URL }}
```

```
service-enable {{ item }} nova-compute
with_items: hypelist.stdout_lines

- name: Confirm instance migration
command: nova --os-username={{ OS_USERNAME }} --os-password={{ OS_
PASSWORD }} --os-tenant-name={{ OS_TENANT_NAME }} --os-auth-url={{
OS_AUTH_URL }}
resize-confirm {{ instance }}

- name: Collect post-migration instance details
shell: nova --os-username={{ OS_USERNAME }} --os-password={{ OS_
PASSWORD }} --os-tenant-name={{ OS_TENANT_NAME }} --os-auth-url={{
OS_AUTH_URL }}
list --name {{ instance }} --fields OS-EXT-SRV-ATTR:host,status | awk
'NR > 3' | awk '{ print $4 " and has a status of " $6 }' | awk 'NR ==
1'
register: postinststat

- name: Show instance location and status
debug: msg="{{ instance }} was migrated from {{ item.0 }} to {{ item.1
}}"
with_together:
- preinststat.stdout_lines
- postinststat.stdout_lines
```

The corresponding variable file named `main.yml`, located in the `instance-migrate/`
`vars` directory, for this role will look similar to the following example:

```
---
desthype: 021579-compute02
instance: testG-2c00131c-c2c7-4eae-aa90-981e54ca7b04
migreason: "Migrating instance to new compute node"
```

Next, the master playbook file named `migrate.yml`, located in the root of the
playbook directory, will look similar to the following example:

```
---
# This playbook used to migrate instance to specific compute node.

- hosts: util_container
user: root
remote_user: root
sudo: yes
roles:
- instance-migrate
```

Following that, we created the `hosts` file, which is also located in the root of the playbook directory:

```
[localhost]
localhostansible_connection=local

[util_container]
172.29.236.199
```

Finally, creating the global variable file named `util_container` and saving it to the `group_vars/` directory of the playbook will complete the playbook:

```
# Here are variables related globally to the util_container host group

OS_USERNAME: ansible
OS_PASSWORD: passwd
OS_TENANT_NAME: admin
OS_AUTH_URL: http://172.29.236.7:35357/v2.0
```

> The complete set of code can again be found in the following GitHub repository:
>
> `https://github.com/os-admin-with-ansible/os-admin-with-ansible`

We have finally landed on my favorite part of creating Ansible playbooks and roles, which is to test out our great work. Fortunately, for you I have knocked out all the bugs already (wink wink). Assuming you have cloned the GitHub repository from the link provided in the note, the command to test the playbook from the `Deployment` node will be as follows:

```
$ cd os-admin-with-ansible
$ ansible-playbook -i hosts migrate.yml
```

A sample of the playbook execution output is as shown in the following screenshot:

```
PLAY [util_container] ********************************************************

GATHERING FACTS *************************************************************
ok: [172.29.236.85]

TASK: [instance-migrate | Retrieve hypervisor list] ************************
changed: [172.29.236.85]

TASK: [instance-migrate | Collect pre-migration instance details] **********
changed: [172.29.236.85]

TASK: [instance-migrate | Disable unselected hypervisors] ******************
changed: [172.29.236.85] => (item=021579-compute01)
changed: [172.29.236.85] => (item=021579-compute03)

TASK: [instance-migrate | Migrate instance] *******************************
changed: [172.29.236.85]

TASK: [instance-migrate | Enable the disabled hypervisors] *****************
changed: [172.29.236.85] => (item=021579-compute01)
changed: [172.29.236.85] => (item=021579-compute03)

TASK: [instance-migrate | Confirm instance migration] *********************
changed: [172.29.236.85]

TASK: [instance-migrate | Collect post-migration instance details] *********
changed: [172.29.236.85]

TASK: [instance-migrate | Show instance location and status] **************
ok: [172.29.236.85] => (item=[u'021579-compute03', u'021579-compute02 and has a status of ACTIVE']) => {
    "item": [
        "021579-compute03",
        "021579-compute02 and has a status of ACTIVE"
    ],
    "msg": "testG-2c00131c-c2c7-4eae-aa98-981e54ca7b04 was migrated from 021579-compute03 to 021579-compute02 and has a status of ACTIVE"
}

PLAY RECAP *****************************************************************
172.29.236.85              : ok=9    changed=7    unreachable=0    failed=0
```

Summary

It's nice to have completed yet another chapter covering real-life OpenStack administrative duties. The more you create playbooks and roles, the faster you will be able to create a new code just by simply reusing the code created earlier for other purposes. Before this book is over, you will have a nice collection of playbooks/roles to reference for future Ansible automation.

Taking a moment to recap this chapter, you will recall that we covered what an instance migration is and why you might want to use this functionality, we reviewed the two possible migration methods — traditional and live-migration — learned how to manually migrate an instance, and also a work-around on how to use traditional migration to migrate an instance to a specific compute node. Lastly, we created the Ansible playbook and role to automate that work-around approach.

The next chapter is near and dear to my heart, as it required me to spend hours perfecting it for a customer I was working with at the time. It even granted me a *Hands-on Labs* talk slot at the OpenStack Summit that was hosted in Vancouver. While it may not be a traditional OpenStack administrative task asked of you, it will help demonstrate the functional power OpenStack natively has around being able to strictly isolate tenants consuming your clouds resources. In the next chapter, we will cover the steps required to implement multi-isolation within your cloud and demonstrate why automating such a complex administrative task is extremely important. Grab another cup of coffee, have a quick stretch, and let's start with *Chapter 7, Setting up Isolated Tenants*.

7
Setting up Isolated Tenants

In this chapter, we will cover the concept of setting up multi-tenant isolation within your OpenStack cloud. Imagine the idea of being able to force strict segregation of your tenants and being able to assign each unshared resource. Well, out-of-the-box OpenStack offers this functionality. This can be accomplished using the combination of the identity, compute and block storage services. We will start this chapter explaining the building blocks of how to set up multi-tenant isolation. Once the concept is clear, we will review the steps required to automate this task. A special emphasis will be placed on explaining how automation of this level prevents incorrect configurations, missed steps, and provides an easily repeatable process. The chapter will end with us creating a fully working Ansible playbook, with roles to configure tenant creation with multi-tenant isolation enabled. In this chapter, we will cover the following topics:

- Multi-tenant isolation explained
- Multi-tenant isolation setup
- Pre-configuration steps
- Tenant configuration steps
- Automation considerations
- Coding the playbook and roles
- Playbook and role review

Multi-tenant isolation explained

I still remember the day when a customer asked me to configure multi-tenant isolation on his/her brand new OpenStack cloud. It was a good 15 minutes of stress and fear, as I had heard of a few horror stories related to it. Anyone who has read the *blueprint* (`https://blueprints.launchpad.net/nova/+spec/multi-tenancy-aggregates`) on this feature will know why I was close to panic mode. While the blueprint is very clear on what is needed configuration wise, I personally knew that it was also no guarantee that all the steps were listed and/or worked, as promised. It was at this point that I decided to make sure whether the steps to do this were first clearly documented and proven before promising anything to the customer.

As mentioned earlier, in order to enable the complete feature the OpenStack identity (Keystone), compute (Nova), and block storage (Cinder) services will be involved. The complete multi-tenant isolation feature covers both computing and block storage resources from being isolated. The folks normally just focus on the computing resource component of this feature. In our case, we will also demonstrate how to include a block storage into the feature.

Before we get too far along, let us define multi-tenant isolation in more detail. Setting up your OpenStack cloud with multi-tenant isolation allows a cloud operator to assign a tenant solely to a new or existing host aggregate. You can then populate that host aggregate with compute nodes that will then be assigned to that tenant only. This in turn allows you to dedicate a set group of compute nodes to a particular tenant, preventing the possibility of having *noisy neighbors* and also adding an additional layer of security/privacy within the cloud. Imagine you have two internal departments, human resources and finance, assigned to their independent tenants. The concern arises that the systems/applications on the finance tenant need to be totally segregated from everyone else consuming cloud resources. So instead of creating a duplicate redundant cloud region, you can set up multi-tenant isolation. This is just one of the many use cases showing why you can leverage this feature.

The same process can also apply to any of the Cinder backend(s) configured on your cloud. You can also segregate those Cinder backend(s) and control which tenant(s) can utilize them. This is done using the built-in Cinder quota functionality part of Cinder and Nova. By creating Cinder quotas, you can restrict or allow access to create volumes on a particular volume type from a tenant.

I will apologize in advance for being redundant in relation to the steps required to set up multi-tenant isolation. It is a necessary evil, as there are a lot of steps and one missed step results in either disabling the ability to spin up instances from that tenant and/or the feature not working as expected. Here is a quick breakdown of the required steps to be taken:

- Add additional Nova scheduling filters
- Configure and enable multiple-storage backends for Cinder
- Create volume type(s)
- Create a new tenant(s) (or use existing ones)
- Create a new host aggregate for the tenant
- Add compute nodes to the host aggregate
- Update the host aggregate metadata to include a tenant filter
- Create a custom flavor to include a tenant filter
- Apply volume type quotas

As shown above, the first step to enable this functionality is adding additional Nova scheduler filters to your cloud. The Nova scheduling filters to be added are called `AggregateInstanceExtraSpecsFilter` and `AggregateMultiTenancyIsolation`. Once that has been completed, you now have technically enabled multi-tenant isolation. Now you have to create the virtual linkage between the tenant and host aggregate. The way this is done within OpenStack is to add metadata tags to certain components. In our case, we will add metadata to the host aggregate and custom flavor that will be created. Nova will use the defined metadata tag called `filter_tenant_id`. This is where you will provide the tenant ID of the tenant you are working to isolate.

At this point, as the cloud consumer, you will add a key to a new or existing custom flavor that will instruct the Nova scheduler when you execute the `nova boot` command, as to which host aggregate the tenant can reserve the resources on. The Nova scheduler will select the appropriate host aggregate and examine the resources available within that group. As long as the resources to accommodate the instance being created are available, the instance will subsequently be placed on that group of compute nodes. So with the computing resources part of the isolation complete, we can now review the block storage component.

In order to truly segregate the block storage available on your OpenStack cloud, you will need to configure and enable multiple-storage backends for Cinder. Cinder lets you add multiple backends to your Cinder configuration. Further details on this capability can be found at: `https://wiki.openstack.org/wiki/Cinder-multi-backend`. This can be a different volume(s) made available to Cinder and/or connecting multiple external share storage devices. The simple configuration by which we can enable this is through setting the `enabled_backends` flag in the `cinder.conf` file. An example of the block to be added to the `cinder.conf` file will be shown in the next section.

After the backends are all set up, you will then create *volume types* associated with them. The volume type creates a direct link to the backend storage. When creating a volume, you will be presented with the option to select from which volume type it will be created. Basically, this means being able to separate the storage backends use. This will then allow us to set volume type restrictions via quotas. As stated earlier, the Cinder quota will restrict or allow access to a particular volume type. This process will be demonstrated further in the next section.

To sum up all the above implementation steps, here is a visual depiction of how it all works:

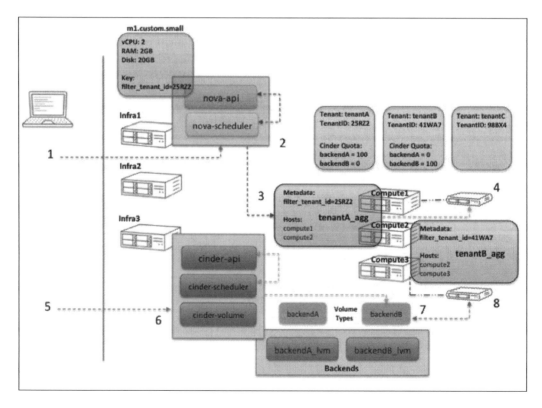

1. The preceding image shows how the end user attached to `tenantA` executes the following CLI request to create an instance:

    ```
    nova boot --flavor m1.custom.small --image cirros-0.3.3
    --security-group default test-instance
    ```

2. The Nova API service then passes the request onto Nova scheduler.

3. As Nova scheduler evaluates the request against the filters enabled, the key (`filter_tenant_id`) injected into the custom flavor selected instructs the scheduler as to which host aggregate this tenant is allowed to utilize.

4. Once the host aggregate is selected (`tenantA_agg`), the scheduler is able to pass the request onto the appropriate compute node to spawn the instance.

5. The end user attached to `tenantB` now executes the following CLI request to create a new volume:

    ```
    cinder create --volume-type backendB --display-name log_vol01 20
    ```

6. The Cinder API service then passes the request onto the Cinder scheduler.

7. The Cinder scheduler will evaluate the backends configured on the cloud; due to passing the additional CLI argument `--volume-type`, it will target the volume creation on the volume-type specified.

8. The volume will now be created on the volume-type named `backend`. The volume can then be mounted to the instance running on host aggregate `tenantB_agg`.

> As a general disclaimer, as per the OpenStack blueprint on multi-tenant isolation, if a compute node does not belong to any host aggregate, then all the tenants can create instances on it. Also, if a compute node belongs to a host aggregate that does not have defined the metadata tag `filter_tenant_id`, all tenants can create instances on it.
>
> In other words, if you apply the multi-tenant isolation filter, you must have all compute nodes in a host aggregate with the `filter_tenant_id` metadata defined in order for it to work properly.
>
> The other fun fact to remember is that each tenant created while the multi-tenant isolation is enabled must be coupled with a new host aggregate with its tenant ID defined. If this is not done, then the new tenant will not be able to create any instances and as per Nova scheduler there will be no available hosts. It is for this reason you must create host aggregates and not availability zones. The availability zones only allow for a compute node to be contained in one availability zone at a time.

Let's now move on to demonstrating the actual implementation steps required to enable multi-tenant isolation in the next section. The process will involve updating OpenStack service configuration files and executing CLI commands.

Setting up multi-tenant isolation

Using the breakdown provided in the previous section, we will now go step-by-step through each configuration, thus showing working configuration examples. The first part will be the pre-configuration steps required just to enable the multi-tenant isolation feature. After that we will then manually demonstrate the specific CLI commands to complete the configuration for a tenant.

Pre-configuration steps

Next, we will outline all the pre-configuration steps required before you can start your multi-tenant isolation setup.

Step 1

As mentioned earlier, probably the most important step is to add the additional Nova scheduler filters, in order to enable multi-tenant isolation. This is done by updating the `nova.conf` file, which is most likely located in the `/etc/nova` directory where the scheduler is installed. The filters to be added are named: `AggregateInstanceExtraSpecsFilter` and `AggregateMultiTenancyIsolation`. The following example is what it should look like once the update is complete:

```
...
scheduler_available_filters = nova.scheduler.filters.all_filters
scheduler_default_filters = AggregateInstanceExtraSpecsFilter,Aggregat
eMultiTenancyIsolation,RetryFilter,AvailabilityZoneFilter,RamFilter,Co
mputeFilter,ComputeCapabilitiesFilter,ImagePropertiesFilter,ServerGrou
pAntiAffinityFilter,ServerGroupAffinityFilter,AggregateCoreFilter,Aggr
egateDiskFilter
scheduler_driver_task_period = 60
...
```

Adding these filters tells Nova to adhere to the host aggregate metadata filter, which we will apply in the next section.

Step 2

If you are not going to extend your multi-tenant isolation capability to the block storage attached to the cloud, you can skip this step; otherwise we will now enable Cinder's multiple-storage functionality by appending additional storage backends to the `enabled_backends` flag, within the `cinder.conf` file. The following is an example of what the configuration block will look similar to:

```
enabled_backends=backendA-lvm,backendB-lvm
[backendA-lvm]
volume_driver=cinder.volume.drivers.lvm.LVMISCSIDriver
volume_backend_name=LVM_iSCSI
volume_group=cinder-volumes

[backendB-lvm]
volume_driver=cinder.volume.drivers.lvm.LVMISCSIDriver
volume_backend_name=LVM_iSCSI_2
volume_group=cinder-volumes2
```

The second component of this step is to create a volume type, which corresponds to the backends configured above. We will have to create two individual volume types if we were to follow the example used here. This is handled using the `cinder type-create` and `cinder type-key` CLI commands. Here is a working example of the commands:

```
$ cinder type-create <volume type name>
```

```
$ cinder type-key <volume type name> set volume_backend_name=<backend
name>
```

A real life working example will look similar to this:

```
$ cinder type-create backendA
$ cinder type-key backendA set volume_backend_name=LVM_iSCSI
```

```
$ cinder type-create backendB
$ cinder type-key backendB set volume_backend_name=LVM_iSCSI_2
```

Now that the pre-configuration steps have been completed, we can move on to outlining the configurations that need to be applied per tenant.

Tenant configuration steps

A cloud operator will need to apply the following process for each tenant being created within an OpenStack cloud, with multi-tenant isolation enabled. Remember that this process can be applied for existing and new tenants created within your OpenStack cloud.

Step 1 – create a new or use an existing tenant

If the tenant you wish to apply multi-tenant isolation to does not exist already, create the tenant using the `keystone tenant-create` CLI command. If the tenant already exists, you just need to record the `tenant ID` associated with it. This task can be accomplished by using the `keystone tenant-get` command. As we mentioned in the previous section, the `tenant ID` will be needed in order to apply the metadata tag on the host aggregate and custom flavor.

Step 2 – create new host aggregate

In this step, you will create a new host aggregate that will be linked to the tenant selected from the preceding section. A host aggregate has the ability to group compute nodes together and the ability to append metadata that is used by Nova scheduler to make the hypervisor selection. The major difference between a host aggregate and an **availability zone (AZ)** is that you can have a compute node that exists in multiple host aggregates. An AZ only allows a compute node to exist in one zone at a time. So, you can create multiple host aggregates and have the same compute nodes exist in each of them. This capability will be needed as each tenant will have to have a host aggregate associated with, it and you may need to overlap compute nodes across multiple tenants. The command to accomplish this is as follows:

```
$ nova aggregate-create <aggregate_name>
```

```
$ nova aggregate-create tenantA-agg
```

The output of the command will resemble the following screenshot:

```
+----+-----------+-------------------+-------+----------+
root@infra1_utility_container-762f6a29:~# nova aggregate-create tenantA-agg
+----+-----------+-------------------+-------+----------+
| Id | Name      | Availability Zone | Hosts | Metadata |
+----+-----------+-------------------+-------+----------+
| 1  | tenantA-agg | -               |       |          |
+----+-----------+-------------------+-------+----------+
```

Make sure to take note of the `aggregateID` of the aggregate you just created. We will need the ID in the next few steps.

Step 3 – add hosts to the new host aggregate

With the host aggregate created, we now have to add hosts to be linked to it. The following command will have to be repeated for every host being added. It is best to use the `aggregateID` from the previous step. My lab environment has three compute nodes and it requires us to execute the command three times. In keeping with our working example, the command will then be:

```
$ nova aggregate-add-host <aggregateID><host_name>
```

```
$ nova aggregate-add-host 1 021579-compute01

$ nova aggregate-add-host 1 021579-compute02

$ nova aggregate-add-host 1 021579-compute03
```

The output of the command will resemble the following screenshot:

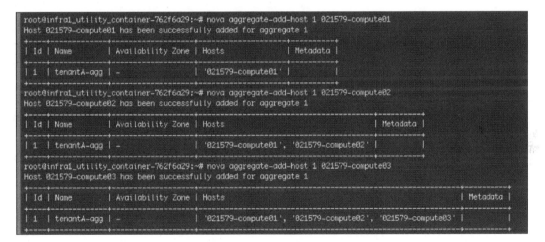

Step 4 – update host aggregate metadata

We are almost done with setting up our host aggregate. The last step related to the host aggregate is to update the metadata associated with it to include a `tenantID` filter. The reason for this filter is to tell Nova scheduler to restrict access to this host aggregate, based on the `tenantID` supplied. At this point, the tenant and host aggregate will be linked together. The working example of the command can be found here:

```
$ nova aggregate-set-metadata <aggregateID> filter_tenant_id=<tenantID>
$ nova aggregate-set-metadata 1 filter_tenant_id=bd7de89923f84fa48208e9bf
3194c694
```

The output of the command will resemble the following screenshot:

Step 5 – create a custom flavor to include the tenant filter

When creating instances from this point forward, you need to make sure that you direct the Nova scheduler to the computing resources you are permitted to consume. The easiest way to accomplish this is to embed the tenant filter into the flavor used to create your instances. In order to make this a seamless process for the cloud consumer, you will have to create custom flavors for each tenant, with their `tenantID` as a key for each flavor. The basic command to create a custom non-shared flavor is as follows:

```
$ nova flavor-create <flavor name> <id> <ram> <disk> <vcpus> --is-public
false
$ nova flavor-create m1.custom.small auto 2000 20 2 --is-public false
```

With the flavor now created, we need to grant the proper tenant access to that flavor. Since this is a custom flavor, just for a specific tenant, we will add a single tenant. The command to accomplish this will look similar to this:

```
$ nova flavor-access-add <flavor name> <tenant ID>
$ nova flavor-access-add m1.custom.small bd7de89923f84fa48208e9bf3194c694
```

The output of the command will resemble the following screenshot:

```
root@infra1_utility_container-762f6a29:~# nova flavor-access-add m1.custom.small  bd7de89923f84fa48208e9bf3194c694
+----------------------------------+----------------------------------+
| Flavor_ID                        | Tenant_ID                        |
+----------------------------------+----------------------------------+
| 01b17f5d-b197-4bcd-bf85-5913ac899981 | bd7de89923f84fa48208e9bf3194c694 |
+----------------------------------+----------------------------------+
```

The final part of this step is to add the `filter_tenant_ID` flavor key to the new custom flavor. Again, the key will direct Nova scheduler to the appropriate host aggregate to allocate the resources when booting the instance. The command to add the flavor key is as follows:

```
$ nova flavor-key <flavor name> set filter_tenant_id=<tenant ID>
```

```
$ nova flavor-key m1.custom.small set filter_tenant_id=bd7de89923f84fa482
08e9bf3194c694
```

This command does not present any output to the screen. In order to check that your changes were implemented as expected, you can execute the `nova flavor-show` command. An example output of this command will look similar to the following screenshot:

```
root@infra1_utility_container-762f6a29:~# nova flavor-key m1.custom.small set filter_tenant_id=bd7de89923f84fa48208e9bf3194c694
root@infra1_utility_container-762f6a29:~# nova flavor-show m1.custom.small
+----------------------------+---------------------------------------------------+
| Property                   | Value                                             |
+----------------------------+---------------------------------------------------+
| OS-FLV-DISABLED:disabled   | False                                             |
| OS-FLV-EXT-DATA:ephemeral  | 0                                                 |
| disk                       | 20                                                |
| extra_specs                | {"filter_tenant_id": "bd7de89923f84fa48208e9bf3194c694"} |
| id                         | 01b17f5d-b197-4bcd-bf85-5913ac899981              |
| name                       | m1.custom.small                                   |
| os-flavor-access:is_public | False                                             |
| ram                        | 2000                                              |
| rxtx_factor                | 1.0                                               |
| swap                       |                                                   |
| vcpus                      | 2                                                 |
+----------------------------+---------------------------------------------------+
```

Note that the `filter_tenant_ID` key has now been added to the custom flavor.

Step 6 – apply volume type quotas

This implementation step is required only if you are going to extend your multi-tenant isolation capability to the block storage attached to the cloud. As we covered in the earlier section of this chapter, the additional Cinder backends were configured/linked to volume types. This is to make sure that you can take advantage of the capability to control access to those volume types. This is where you can enforce the Cinder quota feature, now that volume types are a part of the quota options.

In order to use the Cinder quota feature for our purposes here, we need to set values to allow and restrict access to the volume type. This is because all volume types will be automatically listed as a quota option for all tenants. The following working examples demonstrate the process of updating the default Cinder quotas to allow and restrict access to a particular volume type.

The basic command to update a Cinder based quota to control access to a volume type is as follows:

```
$ cinder quota-update --volumes <# of volumes> --volume-type <volume
type><tenantID>
```

To allow access to a volume type:

```
$ cinder quota-update --volumes 100 --volume-type backendA
bd7de89923f84fa48208e9bf3194c694
```

To restrict access to a volume type:

```
$ cinder quota-update --volumes 0 --volume-type backendA
bd7de89923f84fa48208e9bf3194c694
```

This concludes all the configuration steps needed to completely implement multi-tenant isolation. Looking back at all the required steps and specific configurations reviewed in the preceding section, you should definitely be able to appreciate why automating an administrative task like this is a smart idea. In the next few sections, we will review the required steps to automate this task.

Automation considerations

At this point, we have absorbed a fair amount of framework decisions while creating our Ansible code. There is one new consideration that I want to offer up before getting started.

When stepping into the world of automating administrative tasks, you must always try to wear your system administrator hat. This means being able to think like one and attempt to predict any flexibility that you need to build into your code. Not every task will be an exact replica of the last. Adding the capability to adjust the parameters needed to execute a specific task is extremely helpful for an individual using your automation code. This can be accomplished by adding additional variables within your code and avoiding hard coding command arguments, as much as possible. Yes, there are many good use cases for hard coding items within your code. The point is to try to keep them to a minimum. You should always aim to think out of the box, as much as humanly possible.

Chapter 7

Coding the playbook and roles

In this section, we will create a playbook and role that will set up a tenant to use the enabled multi-tenant isolation functionality within your OpenStack cloud. To leverage this task, you must have completed the pre-configuration steps outlined in the preceding section. We will not cover these steps in the role being created next. However, we will take the steps outlined two sections earlier, automate them so that you only need to supply a few variable values, and then execute only one command.

Before getting started, here is another brief outline of the tasks we will have to do:

1. Create a new tenant.
2. Create new host aggregate.
3. Add hosts to new host aggregate.
4. Update host aggregate metadata.
5. Create custom flavor to include tenant filter.
6. Apply volume type quotas (optional).

In this case we will focus solely on creating a role, we can start with the `main.yml` file within the role directory named `tenant-isolation/tasks`. The initial contents of this file will look similar to the following example:

```
---
- name: Create new tenant
  command: keystone --os-username={{ OS_USERNAME }} --os-password={{
    OS_PASSWORD }} --os-tenant-name={{ OS_TENANT_NAME }} --os-auth-url={{
    OS_AUTH_URL }}
    tenant-create --name={{ tenant_name }} --description="{{ tenant_desc
    }}"

- name: Get new tenant ID
  shell: keystone --os-username={{ OS_USERNAME }} --os-password={{ OS_
    PASSWORD }} --os-tenant-name={{ OS_TENANT_NAME }} --os-auth-url={{
    OS_AUTH_URL }}
    tenant-list | awk '/ {{ tenant_name }} / {print $2}'
  register: tent1
```

The first two tasks are to create a new tenant and then register the tenant ID for later use within the role. Similar to what was done in *Chapter 3, Creating Multiple Users/Tenants*, we use the `keystone tenant-create` command. Once that command is executed, you can issue the `keystone tenant-list` command and strip down the output to provide just the tenant ID. Again, we will do this using the `awk` command and pipe (|) symbol. Remember the `shell` module is used here because we are executing commands that require shell-specific operations.

The next two tasks will create a new host aggregate and then register the `aggregateID` for later use within the role. The code to accomplish this looks similar to this:

```
- name: Create new host aggregate
  command: nova --os-username={{ OS_USERNAME }} --os-password={{ OS_
  PASSWORD }} --os-tenant-name={{ OS_TENANT_NAME }} --os-auth-url={{
  OS_AUTH_URL }}
  aggregate-create {{ agg_name }}

- name: Get new aggregate ID
  shell: nova --os-username={{ OS_USERNAME }} --os-password={{ OS_
  PASSWORD }} --os-tenant-name={{ OS_TENANT_NAME }} --os-auth-url={{
  OS_AUTH_URL }}
  aggregate-list | awk '/ {{ agg_name }} / {print $2}'
  register: aggre1
```

For this task we used the Nova CLI command `nova aggregate-create` to create the new host aggregate. Similar to what we did in the previous tasks, we will then use the `nova aggregate-list` command and the `awk` command to strip out the `aggregateID` from the aggregate just created.

The fifth task will be to add compute nodes to the new host aggregate. Remember, we will have to repeat the following task for each host being added. The code to do this will look similar to this:

```
- name: Add hosts to aggregate, one command for each host using the ID
  from the aggregate just created
  command: nova --os-username={{ OS_USERNAME }} --os-password={{ OS_
  PASSWORD }} --os-tenant-name={{ OS_TENANT_NAME }} --os-auth-url={{
  OS_AUTH_URL }}
  aggregate-add-host {{ aggre1.stdout }} {{ item.name }}
  with_items: compute
```

The `nova aggregate-add-host` command was used to add compute nodes to the host aggregate. The order in which they are added does not matter. For this task, we used a defined variable named `compute`. This variable will provide a list of compute nodes inputted by yourself within the variable file for this role.

Moving on to the sixth task, we will now add the `filter_tenant_id` filter as a metadata tag for the host aggregate. See the following supporting code:

```
- name: Update aggregate metadata to include tenant ID filter
  command: nova --os-username={{ OS_USERNAME }} --os-password={{ OS_
  PASSWORD }} --os-tenant-name={{ OS_TENANT_NAME }} --os-auth-url={{
  OS_AUTH_URL }}
  aggregate-set-metadata {{ aggre1.stdout }} filter_tenant_id={{ tent1.
  stdout }}
```

Technically, at this point the new tenant is configured to utilize the multi-tenant isolation functionality. But for the new tenant to be able to consume resources within the host aggregate allocated for it, we must create a custom flavor, grant access to it from the tenant, and add a specific key to the flavor. The following three tasks will handle this for us:

```
- name: Create custom flavor
command: nova --os-username={{ OS_USERNAME }} --os-password={{ OS_
PASSWORD }} --os-tenant-name={{ OS_TENANT_NAME }} --os-auth-url={{
OS_AUTH_URL }}
flavor-create {{ FLAVOR_NAME }} auto {{ FLAVOR_RAM }} {{ FLAVOR_DISK
}} {{ FLAVOR_CPU }} --is-public false

- name: Grant access to custom flavor for tenant
command: nova --os-username={{ OS_USERNAME }} --os-password={{ OS_
PASSWORD }} --os-tenant-name={{ OS_TENANT_NAME }} --os-auth-url={{
OS_AUTH_URL }}
flavor-access-add {{ FLAVOR_NAME }} {{ tent1.stdout }}

- name: Add flavor key to new flavor
command: nova --os-username={{ OS_USERNAME }} --os-password={{ OS_
PASSWORD }} --os-tenant-name={{ OS_TENANT_NAME }} --os-auth-url={{
OS_AUTH_URL }}
flavor-key {{ FLAVOR_NAME }} set filter_tenant_id={{ tent1.stdout }}
```

The tasks created will utilize most of the variables defined within the variable file for the role. As with the rest of the role, we will reuse the `tenantID` we captured earlier. The `nova flavor-access-add` and `nova flavor-key` commands are two new OpenStack CLI commands that we are introducing here. The purpose of the commands are indicative of their names. With the flavor now configured, the cloud consumer assigned to this tenant will now be able to begin consuming cloud resources.

If you planned to isolate the Cinder controlled storage attached to your cloud, you will need to uncomment the following two final tasks located inside the contents of role. These two tasks will handle the Cinder volume type access demands. Using variables, you will be able to determine which volume types the tenant can have access to. Please find the two additional tasks you will have to add below:

```
- name: Update default Cinder quota to allow volume type access
command: cinder --os-username={{ OS_USERNAME }} --os-password={{ OS_
PASSWORD }} --os-tenant-name={{ OS_TENANT_NAME }} --os-auth-url={{
OS_AUTH_URL }}
quota-update --volumes {{ item.volnum }} --volume-type {{ item.name }}
{{ tent1.stdout }}
with_items: allow_vol_type
```

```
- name: Update default Cinder quota to restrict volume type access
command: cinder --os-username={{ OS_USERNAME }} --os-password={{ OS_
PASSWORD }} --os-tenant-name={{ OS_TENANT_NAME }} --os-auth-url={{
OS_AUTH_URL }}
quota-update --volumes 0 --volume-type {{ item.name }} {{ tent1.stdout
}}
with_items: restrict_vol_type
```

Make sure to update the variable files with the volume types you wish to allow and restrict access to. Those values must be supplied manually. With this approach you will be able to specify the number of volumes allowed per volume type for each tenant (just in case you need it, you're welcome).

As I will always say, this is just my very opinionated approach to setting up a multi-tenant isolation; I am proud to say that it does work as explained, perfectly. Well it is time to celebrate yet again, as you have just completed your fifth OpenStack administration Ansible role. To support this role, we now need to create the variable file that will go along with it. The variable file will be named `main.yml`, which will be located in the `tenant-isolation/vars` directory.

 Note the values defined in the variable file that are intended to be changed before each execution for normal everyday use.

For this role, the variables defined are a bit more extensive. This time around, the role needs more user input in order to complete all the tasks as per your specific needs.

```
---
tenant_name: tenantB
tenant_desc: Tenant B
agg_name: tenantB_agg

compute:
- name: 021579-compute01
- name: 021579-compute03

allow_vol_type:
- name: vol_type1, volnum: 100
- name: vol_type3, volnum: 50

restrict_vol_type:
- name: vol_type2
- name: vol_type4
```

```
flavor_name: m1.custom.small
flavor_ram: 2000
flavor_disk: 20
flavor_cpu: 2
```

Let's take a moment to break down each variable. The summary will be:

```
tenant_name   # name of the new tenant to create

tenant_desc   # description of the new tenant being created

agg_name      # name of the new host aggregate to create

compute     # this value would be the name of the compute node(s) you
wish to add to the host aggregate

allow_vol_type   # a list of volume types the tenant is allowed to
utilize; it is broken down into values, the name of the volume type
(name) and the quota for the number of volumes (volnum)

restrict_vol_type   # a list of volume types the tenant is permitted
from utilizing

flavor_name   # the name of the custom flavor to be created

flavor_ram   # amount of RAM for the flavor (in MB)

flavor_disk   # amount of disk allocated for the flavor (in GB)

flavor_cpu   # the number of vCPUs for the flavor
```

With the variable file completed, we can move on to creating the master playbook file. The file will be named `isolate.yml` and saved to the root of the playbook directory.

The playbook and role names can be anything you choose. Some specific names have been provided here in order to allow you to easily follow along and reference the completed code found in the GitHub repository. The only warning is whatever you decide to name the roles, they must remain uniform when referenced from within the playbook(s).

The contents of the `isolate.yml` file will be:

```
---
# This playbook used to configure Multi-Tenant Isolation.

- hosts: util_container
user: root
remote_user: root
sudo: yes
roles:
- tenant-isolation
```

The summary of this file is as follows:

```
hosts          # the host or host group to execute the playbook against

user           # the user to use when executing the playbook locally

remote_user    # the user to use when executing the playbook on the
remote host(s)

sudo           # will tell Ansible to sudo into the above user on the
remote host(s)          .

roles          # provide a list of roles to execute as part of this
playbook
```

Adding content to our host inventory file and the global variable file was already explained three chapters ago, so we already have that part covered. The values defined earlier will remain the same. The following is a quick recap of how these files are configured.

The `hosts` file in the root of the playbook directory:

```
[localhost]
localhost ansible_connection=local

[util_container]
172.29.236.199
```

The global variable file inside the `group_vars/` directory:

```
# Here are variables related globally to the util_container host group

OS_USERNAME: ansible
OS_PASSWORD: passwd
OS_TENANT_NAME: admin
OS_AUTH_URL: http://172.29.236.7:35357/v2.0
```

Word of caution

Due to the contents of this file, it should be stored as a secure file within whatever code repository you may use to store your Ansible playbooks/ roles. Gaining access to this information could compromise your OpenStack cloud security.

Very cool my friend, you did great yet again! This role was definitely a bit more advanced, but you are an old pro by now so no worries. Keeping with our tradition, we will finish the chapter with a quick review of the playbook and role just created.

Playbook and role review

Let's jump right into examining the role we created, called `tenant-isolation`. The completed role and file named `main.yml` located in the `tenant-isolation/tasks` directory looks similar to this:

```
---
- name: Create new tenant
command: keystone --os-username={{ OS_USERNAME }} --os-password={{
OS_PASSWORD }} --os-tenant-name={{ OS_TENANT_NAME }} --os-auth-url={{
OS_AUTH_URL }}
tenant-create --name={{ tenant_name }} --description="{{ tenant_desc
}}"

- name: Get new tenant ID
shell: keystone --os-username={{ OS_USERNAME }} --os-password={{ OS_
PASSWORD }} --os-tenant-name={{ OS_TENANT_NAME }} --os-auth-url={{
OS_AUTH_URL }}
tenant-list | awk '/ {{ tenant_name }} / {print $2}'
register: tent1

- name: Create new host aggregate
command: nova --os-username={{ OS_USERNAME }} --os-password={{ OS_
PASSWORD }} --os-tenant-name={{ OS_TENANT_NAME }} --os-auth-url={{
OS_AUTH_URL }}
aggregate-create {{ agg_name }}

- name: Get new aggregate ID
shell: nova --os-username={{ OS_USERNAME }} --os-password={{ OS_
PASSWORD }} --os-tenant-name={{ OS_TENANT_NAME }} --os-auth-url={{
OS_AUTH_URL }}
```

```
aggregate-list | awk '/ {{ agg_name }} / {print $2}'
register: aggre1

- name: Add hosts to aggregate, one command for each host using the ID
from the aggregate just created
command: nova --os-username={{ OS_USERNAME }} --os-password={{ OS_
PASSWORD }} --os-tenant-name={{ OS_TENANT_NAME }} --os-auth-url={{
OS_AUTH_URL }}
aggregate-add-host {{ aggre1.stdout }} {{ item.name }}
with_items: compute

- name: Update aggregate metadata to include tenant ID filter
command: nova --os-username={{ OS_USERNAME }} --os-password={{ OS_
PASSWORD }} --os-tenant-name={{ OS_TENANT_NAME }} --os-auth-url={{
OS_AUTH_URL }}
aggregate-set-metadata {{ aggre1.stdout }} filter_tenant_id={{ tent1.
stdout }}

- name: Create custom flavor
command: nova --os-username={{ OS_USERNAME }} --os-password={{ OS_
PASSWORD }} --os-tenant-name={{ OS_TENANT_NAME }} --os-auth-url={{
OS_AUTH_URL }}
flavor-create {{ flavor_name }} auto {{ flavor_ram }} {{ flavor_disk
}} {{ flavor_cpu }} --is-public false

- name: Grant access to custom flavor for tenant
command: nova --os-username={{ OS_USERNAME }} --os-password={{ OS_
PASSWORD }} --os-tenant-name={{ OS_TENANT_NAME }} --os-auth-url={{
OS_AUTH_URL }}
flavor-access-add {{ flavor_name }} {{ tent1.stdout }}

- name: Add flavor key to new flavor
command: nova --os-username={{ OS_USERNAME }} --os-password={{ OS_
PASSWORD }} --os-tenant-name={{ OS_TENANT_NAME }} --os-auth-url={{
OS_AUTH_URL }}
flavor-key {{ flavor_name }} set filter_tenant_id={{ tent1.stdout }}

#- name: Update default Cinder quota to allow volume type access
#   command: cinder --os-username={{ OS_USERNAME }} --os-password={{
OS_PASSWORD }} --os-tenant-name={{ OS_TENANT_NAME }} --os-auth-url={{
OS_AUTH_URL }}
#           quota-update --volumes {{ item.volnum }} --volume-type {{
item.name }} {{ tent1.stdout }}
#   with_items: allow_vol_type
#
```

```
#- name: Update default Cinder quota to restrict volume type access
#  command: cinder --os-username={{ OS_USERNAME }} --os-password={{
OS_PASSWORD }} --os-tenant-name={{ OS_TENANT_NAME }} --os-auth-url={{
OS_AUTH_URL }}
#          quota-update --volumes 0 --volume-type {{ item.name }} {{
tent1.stdout }}
#  with_items: restrict_vol_type
```

The corresponding variable file named `main.yml`, located in the `tenant-isolation/vars` directory, for this role will look similar to this:

```
---
tenant_name: tenantB
tenant_desc: Tenant B
agg_name: tenantB_agg

compute:
- name: 021579-compute01
- name: 021579-compute03

allow_vol_type:
- { name: vol_type1, volnum: 100 }
- { name: vol_type3, volnum: 50 }

restrict_vol_type:
- name: vol_type2
- name: vol_type4

flavor_name: m1.custom.small
flavor_ram: 2000
flavor_disk: 20
flavor_cpu: 2
```

Next, the master playbook file named `isolate.yml`, located in the root of the playbook directory, will look similar to this:

```
---
# This playbook used to configure Multi-Tenant Isolation.

- hosts: util_container
user: root
remote_user: root
sudo: yes
roles:
- tenant-isolation
```

Following that we created the `hosts` file, which is also located in the root of the playbook directory.

```
[localhost]
localhost ansible_connection=local

[util_container]
172.29.236.199
```

Finally, creating the global variable file named `util_container` and saving it to the `group_vars/` directory of the playbook will complete the playbook.

```
# Here are variables related globally to the util_container host group

OS_USERNAME: ansible
OS_PASSWORD: passwd
OS_TENANT_NAME: admin
OS_AUTH_URL: http://172.29.236.7:35357/v2.0
```

The complete set of code can again be found in the following GitHub repository `https://github.com/os-admin-with-ansible/os-admin-with-ansible`.

Testing out this new playbook and role may be a bit of a challenge; if you are not already set up with multi-tenant isolation enabled, then make sure to give it a try when and if the scenario arises for you. Assuming that you have cloned the GitHub repository earlier, the command to test out the playbook from the `Deployment` node is as follows:

```
$ cd os-admin-with-ansible
$ ansible-playbook -i hosts isolate.yml
```

Summary

Crossing the finish line does feel nice for sure. I am hoping that the raw power of multi-tenant isolation was explained and demonstrated in this chapter. Always feels good to have options, in order to meet your cloud consumer demands. Before concluding this chapter, let's take a moment to recap this chapter:

- We explained what multi-tenant isolation and possible use cases within OpenStack

- We stepped through the setup process for multi-tenant isolation

- We demonstrated the tenant configurations needed after multi-tenant isolation is enabled on your cloud

- We developed an Ansible playbook and role to automate migrating an instance to a specific compute node using the nova migrate command

The next chapter also will be a very interesting one, as a cloud operator you will have hypervisor failures and will have to do maintenance, eventually. In order to successfully handle both of those tasks, you will have to evacuate instances from your compute nodes. Of course, you can do this manually, but why would you? In the next chapter, we will cover the steps required to manually evacuate a compute node within your OpenStack cloud and then take it up a notch with automating this task to be on-demand on a per tenant basis. If you are ready for uncharted waters, set course for *Chapter 8, Deploying OpenStack Features*.

8
Deploying OpenStack Features

In this chapter, we will review a few possible approaches to adding new or existing features to your OpenStack cloud. The power of OpenStack is in the many capabilities that exist within the many OpenStack projects that make up the ecosystem. Some examples of these features can be seen in the different hypervisors supported by Nova, network plugins created for Neutron from many of the network device providers, and the storage drivers available that can be added to your Cinder configuration. Of course, there are many more features that can be easily enabled. Since we have to start somewhere, it felt best to cover one of the most asked-about features of Nova, the multiple hypervisor support. We will also go through the process of enabling a secondary hypervisor type. For our exercise here, we will cover the steps need to deploy Docker as a hypervisor on to your OpenStack cloud. I decided to pick a very popular hypervisor this time, in order to show relevance as to why one should consider this feature (and because I love a challenge). As with all the previous chapters, we will be creating a fully working Ansible playbook that will implement all the configurations to set up Docker as a compute node. In this chapter, we will cover the following topics:

- Multiple hypervisor support
- What is Docker?
- Setting up Docker and nova-docker
- Docker configuration
- Configuring nova-docker
- Coding the playbook and roles
- Playbook and role review

Multiple hypervisor support

This topic happens to be one of my favorites because I love to see the shocked faces of most folks when I say "*OpenStack is not a hypervisor*". Yes, I repeat, "*OpenStack is NOT a hypervisor*". It has to be said twice in order to make sure that the point is being driven home. A very common misunderstanding in reference to OpenStack is that it will be directly compared to other hypervisors that are popular in the market. I am not going to name them, but most of us know what/who I am referring to. From a base level, this type of comparison is similar to literally comparing apples and oranges. One of the first principles that should be made clear when working with OpenStack is that it should be seen more as a hardware and hypervisor manager. The role OpenStack has regarding the hypervisor is to manage the hypervisor's functions and report on its health. OpenStack does not honestly care which hypervisor is made available, as long as there is a code to support that particular system. Inside the OpenStack community, a favorite or default hypervisor was selected, which is KVM; however, this has no bearing on utilizing the other options made available. YOU have options!

At the time this book was published, the following hypervisors were supported:

- KVM (libvirt)
- Hyper-V
- VMware
- XenServer
- Docker
- LXC via libvirt

More details on the OpenStack-supported hypervisors and their testing status can be found at `https://wiki.openstack.org/wiki/HypervisorSupportMatrix`. Please keep in mind that each hypervisor will provide varying features within your cloud and all hypervisors do not have the same OpenStack features available. Take time to review the *Nova Hypervisor Support Matrix*, found at the preceding link, in detail.

Now, let's focus on the hypervisor we have selected for this example. We will first explain some of Docker's hypervisor-like features at a very very high level, just in case you are not familiar, and cover some additional considerations around the *nova-docker* configuration.

What is Docker (aka Docker Engine)?

Just in case you are new to technology as a whole or have not lived among humans for the past 2-3 years I will do my best to explain what Docker is.

Docker is an open source project similar to OpenStack and Ansible, which streamlines the deployment of applications inside the software containers.

Docker can at times be likened to other virtualization software but with much less overhead. Docker basically will add an abstraction layer between the container(s) and the bare metal Linux kernel, allowing the container to run on any Linux server and enabling process isolation. Once your application is deployed within the container, that container can then run on any Linux server where Docker is configured, thus adding a whole new level of portability, flexibility, and encapsulation to your application deployment process.

Docker is governed by a simple API, which is used to manage the containers created. The containers do not require an operating system, but rather utilize the base server's kernel functionality in an isolated fashion. Feel free to dive deeper into Docker by visiting their website at `www.docker.com`. It is well worth the time investment.

Setting up Docker and nova-docker

Using Docker as a hypervisor always made perfect sense to me. The ability to launch pre-defined containers using a centralized API/CLI-driven platform, such as OpenStack, just works. Similar to Kubernetes (of course Kubernetes has a slightly different approach to managing the containers), OpenStack will keep track of your containers across multiple Docker hosts. The power of having the option to do traditional cloud virtualization with KVM right alongside a cluster of Docker nodes speaks of the flexibility OpenStack offers to a cloud operator: no more having to choose one or the other.

In this section, we will review the manual steps to set up Docker and nova-docker within your OpenStack cloud. A brief snapshot of the steps is outlined, as follows:

1. Install Docker on a new compute node(s).
2. Install nova-docker on the compute node(s) (the commit version pulled is very specific and important if running Juno/Kilo).
3. Update the Nova `compute_driver` parameter.
4. Add the `docker.filters` file to the Nova `rootwrap.d` folder.

5. Add the `AggregateInstanceExtraSpecsFilter` filter to the Nova scheduler.

6. Remove the `ComputeCapabilitiesFilter`, `AggregateCoreFilter`, and `AggregateDiskFilter` filters from the Nova scheduler.

7. Create a custom Docker flavor with extra specs.

8. Create a new host aggregate for the Docker compute node(s).

9. Add Docker to the Glance API `container_formats`.

Now, let's go step by step through each configuration step shown in the preceding section, demonstrating the working configuration examples.

Docker configuration

The next steps will now involve installing the Docker packages and all the dependent OpenStack integrations, known as nova-docker, for them to work together. The following section instructs you how to do this.

Install Docker on a new compute node

Installing Docker on a Linux server is actually very easy, and as Docker matures the process simplifies even more. I have chosen to install Docker in a bit of an old-school method. The instructions on the Docker website have changed a bit since I originally attempted this; the good news is my method still works. Feel free to change the install approach later within your role, if you want.

We will install Docker using the `wget` command, as shown:

```
$ wget -qO- https://get.docker.com/ | sh
```

After the installation is complete, it is wise to verify the Docker installation by issuing the following command:

```
$ docker run hello-world
```

The output of this command will look similar to the following screenshot:

```
root@021579-compute04:~# docker run hello-world

Hello from Docker.
This message shows that your installation appears to be working correctly.

To generate this message, Docker took the following steps:
 1. The Docker client contacted the Docker daemon.
 2. The Docker daemon pulled the "hello-world" image from the Docker Hub.
 3. The Docker daemon created a new container from that image which runs the
    executable that produces the output you are currently reading.
 4. The Docker daemon streamed that output to the Docker client, which sent it
    to your terminal.

To try something more ambitious, you can run an Ubuntu container with:
 $ docker run -it ubuntu bash

Share images, automate workflows, and more with a free Docker Hub account:
 https://hub.docker.com

For more examples and ideas, visit:
 https://docs.docker.com/userguide/
```

The final step in the installation process is adding the Nova user to the Docker user group so that the Nova user can manage the Docker functionality. In essence, enabling OpenStack to manage Docker is similar to any other hypervisor. Since we are using a cloud deployed using the OpenStack Ansible (OSAD) method on top of Ubuntu, the appropriate command is:

```
$ usermod –aGdockernova
```

Now with Docker installed, we can move onto the next step of installing the OpenStack integration packages, known as nova-docker. The nova-docker package will tie your new Docker node to OpenStack Nova within your cloud, so that it can be used as a hypervisor.

Configuring nova-docker

The name of this feature is pretty self-explanatory, as it provides the integration between Docker and the OpenStack Compute service (Nova). The installation process for this feature is also very straightforward. It will involve installing Docker drivers for Nova, updates to the Nova configuration files, adding/removing the Nova scheduler filters, creating custom flavors, new host aggregates, and updating the Glance API configuration parameters.

Step 1 – install nova-docker

We will use git to download the drivers on the compute node selected to run Docker, and then check out a specific patch that fixes functionality for the Juno/Kilo release of OpenStack, and finally we will install the driver on the compute node.

We will move into the /opt directory and then issue the following command to pull down the nova-docker drivers:

```
$ cd /opt
$ git clone http://github.com/stackforge/nova-docker.git
```

Next, we have to go pick up the OpenStack patch:

```
$ cd /opt/nova-docker
$ git checkout -b pre-i18n d1ad84793b7f2182de04df8a5323d6928af672ca
```

The final part of this step is to install the nova-docker feature. The nova-docker package is installed via pip from inside the /opt/nova-docker directory:

```
$ pip install
```

Step 2 – update the Nova compute_driver parameter

In this step, we will notify the new compute node via the nova.conf file that it has the capability to utilize the nova-docker feature as a hypervisor. You need to update the nova.conf file, most likely located in the /etc/nova directory. The compute_ driver parameter needs to be updated as follows:

```
compute_driver=novadocker.virt.docker.DockerDriver
```

The following additional configuration parameters should be added to the nova. conf file as well:

```
[docker]
# Commented out. Uncomment these if you'd like to customize:
vif_driver=novadocker.virt.docker.vifs.DockerGenericVIFDriver
## snapshots_directory=/var/tmp/my-snapshot-tempdir
```

After updating the configuration file, you will have to restart the nova-compute service on the compute node.

Step 3 – add the docker.filters file to the Nova rootwrap.d folder

Next, we will add a new filter file named docker.filters inside the /etc/nova/ rootwrap.d directory in order to enable the networking capability for the Docker compute node.

The contents of the file will look similar to this:

```
# nova-rootwrap command filters for setting up network in the docker
driver
# This file should be owned by (and only-writeable by) the root user

[Filters]
# nova/virt/docker/driver.py: 'ln', '-sf', '/var/run/netns/.*'
ln: CommandFilter, /bin/ln, root
```

Step 4 – add and remove filters on the compute node(s) Nova scheduler

Similar to the steps taken in the previous chapters to add the additional Nova scheduler filters, we will update the `nova.conf` file. The filter to be added is named `AggregateInstanceExtraSpecsFilter`.

The small difference in this step is that we will be removing three filters from the scheduler. The Nova scheduler filters can cause a conflict among themselves when adding new filters and enabling certain OpenStack features. This process can be sort of a trial and error type of scenario. Based on the error output from the scheduler, you can troubleshoot the filters that are conflicting with one another. Fortunately, the smart folks of the OpenStack community have figured out some of this for us.

You need to remove the following Nova scheduler filters: `ComputeCapabilitiesFilter`, `AggregateCoreFilter`, and `AggregateDiskFilter`. You will note that removing these filters can potentially break some features that you might be utilizing within your OpenStack cloud. Personally, I did not run into any issues and still had all the commonly-used Nova capabilities within the cloud. You need to make sure to evaluate whether you can safely remove these filters.

Once the updates are complete, it looks similar to the following example:

```
...
scheduler_available_filters = nova.scheduler.filters.all_filters
scheduler_default_filters = AggregateInstanceExtraSpecsFilter,
RetryFilter,AvailabilityZoneFilter,RamFilter,ComputeFilter,ImagePrope
rtiesFilter,ServerGroupAntiAffinityFilter,ServerGroupAffinityFilter
scheduler_driver_task_period = 60
...
```

Step 5 – add and remove filters on the controller node(s) Nova scheduler

In this step, you will repeat the actions executed in step 4 for the Nova scheduler on the controller node(s). The scheduler configurations must match in order for the feature to work correctly.

You will also need to add the additional configuration parameters found in step 2 to the nova.conf file on the controller node(s). For clarity's sake, the new parameters added to the nova.conf file will match the following example:

```
[docker]
# Commented out. Uncomment these if you'd like to customize:
vif_driver=novadocker.virt.docker.vifs.DockerGenericVIFDriver
## snapshots_directory=/var/tmp/my-snapshot-tempdir
```

Step 6 – create a custom Docker flavor with extra specs

In order to notify the Nova scheduler that the instance being created is actually a Docker container, we will need to create a custom flavor with extra specs. This will allow the cloud consumer to easily use this new capability. The basic command to create a custom shared flavor is as follows:

```
$ nova flavor-create <flavor name> <id> <ram> <disk> <vcpus>
$ nova flavor-create m1.custom.small auto 2048 20 1
```

With the flavor now created, we need to append the extra specs to it in order to be able to identify the virt_type (hypervisor) in which the instance using this flavor should be sent to. Note that in the earlier steps we configured our new Docker compute node to know that it was a specific hypervisor type (Docker); adding this extra spec creates the linkage between an instance using this custom flavor and the Docker compute node. The command to add the extra spec needed here will look similar to the following example:

```
$ nova flavor-key <flavor name> set virt_type=docker
$ nova flavor-key m1.custom.small set virt_type=docker
```

This command does not present any output to the screen. In order to check that your changes were implemented as you expected, you can execute the `nova flavor-show` command. An example output of this command looks as shown in the following screenshot:

```
root@infra1_utility_container-762f6a29:~# nova flavor-show m1.container
+----------------------------+------------------------+
| Property                   | Value                  |
+----------------------------+------------------------+
| OS-FLV-DISABLED:disabled   | False                  |
| OS-FLV-EXT-DATA:ephemeral  | 0                      |
| disk                       | 20                     |
| extra_specs                | {"virt_type": "docker"} |
| id                         | m1dockerctr            |
| name                       | m1.container           |
| os-flavor-access:is_public | True                   |
| ram                        | 2048                   |
| rxtx_factor                | 1.0                    |
| swap                       |                        |
| vcpus                      | 1                      |
+----------------------------+------------------------+
```

Step 7 – create a new host aggregate for the Docker compute node(s)

In this step, you will create a new host aggregate that will contain compute nodes configured to run Docker as a hypervisor. In this case, we will also create a matching **availability zone (AZ)** as it is best to logically separate the different hypervisor types. You will then end up with two availability zones, one containing KVM based compute nodes and one containing Docker based compute nodes. The first AZ (called Nova) already exists, as it is a default configuration when installing OpenStack. The command to create the second new host aggregate/AZ is as shown:

```
$ nova aggregate-create <aggregate_name> <az_name>
```

```
$ nova aggregate-create docker docker-zone
```

The next part of the step related to the host aggregate is to update the metadata associated with it to include the `virt_type` filter. This adds the flag needed to tell the Nova scheduler to place the instance only on the compute node part of this host aggregate. The working example of the command can be found here:

```
$ nova aggregate-set-metadata <aggregateID> virt_type=docker
```

```
$ nova aggregate-set-metadata 13 virt_type=docker
```

The last part of this step is to add host(s) to the new host aggregate. The following command will have to be repeated for every host being added. It is best to use the `aggregateID` from the previous step. For my lab environment, I have added one additional compute node configured with Docker and nova-docker. In keeping with our working example, the command will be:

```
$ nova aggregate-add-host <aggregateID> <host_name>
$ nova aggregate-add-host 13 021579-compute04
```

Once all the preceding tasks of this step have been completed, you can issue the `nova aggregate-details` command to confirm your configuration. The output of the command will resemble the following screenshot:

```
root@infra1_utility_container-762f6a29:~# nova aggregate-details docker
+----+--------+-------------------+--------------------+---------------------------------------------------+
| Id | Name   | Availability Zone | Hosts              | Metadata                                          |
+----+--------+-------------------+--------------------+---------------------------------------------------+
| 13 | docker | docker-zone       | '021579-compute04' | 'availability_zone=docker-zone', 'virt_type=docker' |
+----+--------+-------------------+--------------------+---------------------------------------------------+
```

Step 8 – add docker to the Glance API container_formats

The last step involves updating the `glance-api.conf` file located most likely in the `/etc/glance` directory where Glance is installed. We need to add a list of expected image formats to the Glance configuration. Without adding this parameter, Glance will only accept the default image formats, which do not include Docker containers. Add the following line of code inside the `[DEFAULT]` section of the configuration file:

```
container_formats=ami,ari,aki,bare,ovf,ova,docker
```

When you are done, the `glance-api.conf` file should look similar to the following code:

```
[DEFAULT]
container_formats=ami,ari,aki,bare,ovf,ova,docker
verbose = True
debug = False
...
```

At this point, your new Docker compute node(s) are ready to go and the other corresponding OpenStack services now know how to handle requests regarding Docker containers. The effectiveness of automating something similar to this comes into play when you have to repeat the process once more, 10 more times, or even possibly 100 more times. In the next section, we will review the required steps to automate this process.

Coding the playbook and roles

In this section, we will now create the playbooks and roles to add the OpenStack feature of provisioning Docker compute node(s) as a hypervisor to your cloud. When creating Ansible automation code for something of this nature, I typically like to create multiple tasks broken up into separate roles. This format allows you to reuse the roles created with other playbooks. We will end up with four playbooks and six roles to automate the steps outlined in the previous section. Each role will be broken up into its own area within this section of the chapter. At the end, we will recap the playbooks consuming those roles.

Install Docker

The first role that we will create will include the tasks needed to install Docker on the new compute node(s). The name of the file will be `main.yml` located within the role directory named `install-docker/tasks`. The contents of this file will be as shown:

```
---

- name: Install additional packages
apt: name={{item}} state=present
with_items:
    - git
    - wget

- name: Pull down and install Docker packages
shell: chdir=/opt wget -qO- https://get.docker.com/ | sh

- name: Verify the Docker install
command: docker run hello-world

- name: Add Nova user to Docker group
command: usermod -aGdocker nova
```

The first task will install the additional packages needed (if not already present) for the other tasks that are a part of this role or others; the `git` and `wget` packages are needed to add this feature. The second task is meant to download and install the Docker packages onto the compute node(s). The next two tasks will first test the Docker installation, and whether it can successfully add the Nova user to the Docker user group on the compute node(s).

nova-docker

The next role to be created will handle the tasks of installing the `nova-docker` package onto the new compute node(s). Just as with the previous role, the file will be named `main.yml` and located within the role directory name `nova-docker/tasks`. The contents of this file will be similar to the following example:

```
---

- name: Pull down nova-docker package
command: chdir=/opt git clone http://github.com/stackforge/nova-docker.git

- name: Check out nova-docker branch pre-i18n
command: chdir=/opt/nova-dockergit checkout -b pre-i18n
d1ad84793b7f2182de04df8a5323d6928af672ca

- name: Install nova-docker package
command: chdir=/opt/nova-docker pip install
```

This role begins with a task that will clone the **GitHub** repository where the `nova-docker` package is located. The next role handles the checking of a specific patch related to the package. Lastly, the final task will install the `nova-docker` package using `pip`.

nova-update

This role will take care of the OpenStack service-specific configuration adjustments on the new compute node(s). The file will be named `main.yml` within the role directory named `nova-update/tasks`. The initial contents of this file will be as follows:

```
---

- name: Copy Docker filter file
copy: src=docker.filtersdest=/etc/nova/rootwrap.d mode=0644
```

Since this is our first time using the copy module for Ansible, I felt that we should pause here to break down what the preceding task will do. The copy module enables us to copy files locally to the remote location where the role is being executed. I am personally very fond of this module, as it can be a royal pain moving the pre-configured files to various remote locations. The best part of this module and Ansible is that you can then store the file to be moved within the role directory in another directory named files. Earlier, in Chapter 2, *An Introduction to Ansible*, we discussed the role directory structure. The files directory is where you can store files of any format that will be moved by the copy module.

This task will pick up the file named docker.filters and copy it to the /etc/nova/rootwrap.d directory on new compute node(s). The other tasks that are a part of this role are as follows:

```
- name: Change default scheduler filters
shell: chdir=/bin sed -i 's/^scheduler_default_filters.*/scheduler_
default_filters = AggregateInstanceExtraSpecsFilter,RetryFilter,
AvailabilityZoneFilter,RamFilter,ComputeFilter,ImagePropertiesFilter,
ServerGroupAntiAffinityFilter,ServerGroupAffinityFilter/' /etc/nova/
nova.conf

- name: Update Nova compute driver
shell: chdir=/bin sed -i 's/^compute_driver.*/compute_driver
=novadocker.virt.docker.DockerDriver/' /etc/nova/nova.conf
```

The preceding tasks handle updating the nova.conf file using the sed command. The sed command is defined to be a stream editor that can be used to perform simple text transformations on a file. In these two tasks, we did a search for a specific text inside of the nova.conf file and replaced the line with a new line designated in the command.

The next two tasks will then copy a file containing a pre-defined parameter block to the compute node(s) and then append that parameter block onto the end of the nova.conf file. The code used to accomplish this looks similar to the following example:

```
- name: Copy Docker section file
copy: src=dockerdest=/usr/share mode=0644

- name: Insert Docker section into Nova config
shell: chdir=/usr/share cat /usr/share/docker>> /etc/nova/nova.conf
notify: restart nova-compute
```

Again, we will use the `copy` module for Ansible to move the file containing the parameter block to the compute node(s). Now that the file is copied to the node, we can use that file in the next task with the `cat` command. As a part of the last task, we have included a hat trick to restart the nova-compute service once the task is completed. This is accomplished using the `notify` action included within the playbooks/roles. The action will be triggered at the end of each block of tasks and is only executed once, no matter how many times it is called from other tasks.

The last line of the task will trigger an action to call the `main.yml` file located within the handler's directory of the role. The contents of this file will include a pointer to the triggered action called `nova-compute`. The following are the contents of this file:

```
---
- name: restart nova-compute
  service: name=nova-compute state=restarted
```

openstack-config

For this role, we will create the custom flavor and host aggregate dedicated to the Docker compute node(s). As reviewed earlier, these new items will have extra metadata associated with them in order to inform the Nova scheduler how to handle them when executed. The file will be named `main.yml` within the role directory name `openstack-config/tasks`.

For these tasks, we used the Nova CLI commands `nova flavor-create`, `nova flavor-key`, `nova aggregate-create`, and `nova aggregate-set-metadata` to complete the required actions. The code to do this will look similar to this:

```
---

- name: Create new instance flavor for Docker
command: nova --os-username={{ OS_USERNAME }} --os-password={{ OS_
PASSWORD }} --os-tenant-name={{ OS_TENANT_NAME }} --os-auth-url={{ OS_
AUTH_URL }} flavor-create {{ FLAVOR_NAME }} {{ FLAVOR_ID }} 2048 20 1

- name: Define extra specs for Docker flavor
command: nova --os-username={{ OS_USERNAME }} --os-password={{ OS_
PASSWORD }} --os-tenant-name={{ OS_TENANT_NAME }} --os-auth-url={{
OS_AUTH_URL }} flavor-key {{ FLAVOR_ID }} set virt_type=docker

- name: Create new Host Aggregate for Docker nodes
command: nova --os-username={{ OS_USERNAME }} --os-password={{ OS_
PASSWORD }} --os-tenant-name={{ OS_TENANT_NAME }} --os-auth-url={{
OS_AUTH_URL }} aggregate-create {{ AGG_NAME }} {{ AVAIL_ZONE }}
```

```
- name: Create new Host Aggregate for Docker nodes
command: nova --os-username={{ OS_USERNAME }} --os-password={{ OS_
PASSWORD }} --os-tenant-name={{ OS_TENANT_NAME }} --os-auth-url={{
OS_AUTH_URL }} aggregate-set-metadata {{ AGG_NAME }} virt_type=docker
```

The unique part of the commands discussed in the preceding section relates mainly to the `nova flavor-key` and `nova aggregate-set-metadata` commands. You will notice that we are setting special metadata parameters related to setting up these new compute node(s) as Docker hypervisors. Setting the `virt_type=docker` metadata is the linkage needed to direct the Nova scheduler to the correct compute node(s) when this specific flavor is used.

nova-scheduler

The tasks outlined in this role almost exactly match those described for the `nova-update` role created in the earlier section. The difference is that this role will be run against the Nova scheduler container running on the control plane instead of the new compute node(s). Note that the changes in the Nova scheduler filter need to match with the Nova scheduler and the compute node(s). This role will handle keeping them in sync. The file will be named `main.yml` within the role directory named `nova-scheduler/tasks`.

```
---

- name: Change default scheduler filters
shell: chdir=/bin sed -i 's/^scheduler_default_filters.*/scheduler_
default_filters = AggregateInstanceExtraSpecsFilter,RetryFilter,
AvailabilityZoneFilter,RamFilter,ComputeFilter,ImagePropertiesFilter,
ServerGroupAntiAffinityFilter,ServerGroupAffinityFilter/' /etc/nova/
nova.conf

- name: Copy Docker section file
copy: src=dockerdest=/usr/share mode=0644

- name: Insert Docker section into Nova config
shell: chdir=/usr/share cat /usr/share/docker>> /etc/nova/nova.conf
notify: restart nova-scheduler
```

glance-update

This last and final role will add the list of image formats Glance should expect/ support. If we do not add this, Glance will use the default image formats. Since Docker is not considered a default image format, the build of your container will fail. This is why we have to add a pre-defined list of formats to the Glance API configuration file. The file will be named `main.yml` within the role directory named `glance-update/tasks`.

```
---

- name: Add container formats to Glance API config file
  shell: chdir=/bin sed -i '/^\[DEFAULT/a container_formats=ami,ari,aki,
bare,ovf,ova,docker' /etc/glance/glance-api.conf
  notify: restart glance-api
```

One word of caution is that Docker is new, even newer than OpenStack, and could at times stop working with the nova-docker drivers. What can I say? It is one of the causalities of open source software; for better and for worse. Do not worry, you get used to it but I will always encourage you not to give up and find a way to get it to work. Yes, it is officially the time to celebrate again, as you have just completed your sixth OpenStack administration Ansible role.

To support these roles, we now need to create the variable file that will go along with it. For this series of roles, we will use a global variable file to simplify things a bit. The file will be named `util_container` and we will be saving it to the `group_vars/` directory of the playbook.

Keep in mind that the values defined in the variable file are intended to be changed before each execution for normal everyday use.

The variables defined in the following section should look very familiar at this point. The standard variables needed to authenticate your OpenStack cloud and the other OpenStack configurations requiring user input exist here.

```
# Here are variables related to the nova-docker setup

OS_USERNAME: admin
OS_PASSWORD: passwd
OS_TENANT_NAME: admin
OS_AUTH_URL: http://172.29.236.7:35357/v2.0
FLAVOR_NAME: m1.container
FLAVOR_ID: m1dockerctr
AGG_NAME: docker
AVAIL_ZONE: docker-zone
```

Word of caution

Due to the contents of this file, it should be stored as a secure file within the code repository that you may use to store your Ansible playbooks/ roles. Gaining access to this information might compromise your OpenStack cloud security.

Let's take a moment to break down the new variables. The summary will be:

```
FLAVOR_NAME  # the name of the custom flavor to be created

FLAVOR_ID  # the ID associated with the custom flavor

AGG_NAME     # name of the new host aggregate to create

AVAIL_ZONE   # the zone name associated with the new host aggregate
```

With the variable file completed, we can now move on to creating the master playbook files. For our demonstration, I decided to break up the playbook files into separate files. This was totally my choice and could be combined into one file with no issues. The list of playbook files will be described, as follows:

```
base.yml
install-docker
nova-docker
nova-update

base-openstack.yml
openstack-config

base-scheduler.yml
nova-scheduler

base-glance.yml
glance-update
```

The playbook and role names can be anything you choose. Specific names have been provided here in order to allow you to easily follow along and reference the complete code found in the GitHub repository. The only warning being that whatever you decide to name them, the roles must remain uniform when referenced from within the playbook(s).

Since adding this feature to OpenStack involved adjustment to more services, we needed to add additional hosts to our host inventory file. The following is a quick recap of how these files are configured.

The `hosts` file in the root of the playbook directory is:

```
[docker_nodes]
021579-docker02

[util_container]
172.29.236.179

[nova_schedulers]
172.29.236.218

[glance_container]
172.29.236.115
```

Well done everyone, you just added Docker to your OpenStack cloud. This was one of my favorite features to add so far, outside of configuring Trove. As always, for us to keep up with our tradition, we will finish up the chapter with a quick review of the playbook and role just created.

Playbook and role review

Let's jump right into examining the roles we created.

The completed role and file named `main.yml` located in the `install-docker/tasks` directory looks similar to this:

```
---

- name: Install additional packages
apt: name={{item}} state=present
with_items:
    - git
    - wget

- name: Pull down and install Docker packages
shell: chdir=/opt wget -qO- https://get.docker.com/ | sh

- name: Verify the Docker install
command: docker run hello-world

- name: Add Nova user to Docker group
command: usermod -aGdocker nova
```

The completed role and file named `main.yml` located in the `nova-docker/tasks` directory looks as follows:

```
---

- name: Pull down nova-docker package
command: chdir=/opt git clone http://github.com/stackforge/nova-docker.git

- name: Check out nova-docker branch pre-i18n
command: chdir=/opt/nova-dockergit checkout -b pre-i18n
d1ad84793b7f2182de04df8a5323d6928af672ca

- name: Install nova-docker package
command: chdir=/opt/nova-docker pip install
```

The completed role and file named `main.yml` located in the `nova-update/tasks` directory looks similar to the following example:

```
---

- name: Copy Docker filter file
copy: src=docker.filtersdest=/etc/nova/rootwrap.d mode=0644

- name: Change default scheduler filters
shell: chdir=/bin sed -i 's/^scheduler_default_filters.*/scheduler_
default_filters = AggregateInstanceExtraSpecsFilter,RetryFilter,
AvailabilityZoneFilter,RamFilter,ComputeFilter,ImagePropertiesFilter,
ServerGroupAntiAffinityFilter,ServerGroupAffinityFilter/' /etc/nova/
nova.conf

- name: Update Nova compute driver
shell: chdir=/bin sed -i 's/^compute_driver.*/compute_driver =
novadocker.virt.docker.DockerDriver/' /etc/nova/nova.conf

- name: Copy Docker section file
copy: src=dockerdest=/usr/share mode=0644

- name: Insert Docker section into Nova config
shell: chdir=/usr/share cat /usr/share/docker>> /etc/nova/nova.conf
notify: restart nova-compute
```

The completed role and file named `main.yml` located in the `openstack-config/
tasks` directory looks similar to the following example:

```
---

- name: Create new instance flavor for Docker
command: nova --os-username={{ OS_USERNAME }} --os-password={{ OS_
PASSWORD }} --os-tenant-name={{ OS_TENANT_NAME }} --os-auth-url={{ OS_
AUTH_URL }} flavor-create {{ FLAVOR_NAME }} {{ FLAVOR_ID }} 2048 20 1

- name: Define extra specs for Docker flavor
command: nova --os-username={{ OS_USERNAME }} --os-password={{ OS_
PASSWORD }} --os-tenant-name={{ OS_TENANT_NAME }} --os-auth-url={{
OS_AUTH_URL }} flavor-key {{ FLAVOR_ID }} set virt_type=docker

- name: Create new Host Aggregate for Docker nodes
command: nova --os-username={{ OS_USERNAME }} --os-password={{ OS_
PASSWORD }} --os-tenant-name={{ OS_TENANT_NAME }} --os-auth-url={{
OS_AUTH_URL }} aggregate-create {{ AGG_NAME }} {{ AVAIL_ZONE }}

- name: Create new Host Aggregate for Docker nodes
command: nova --os-username={{ OS_USERNAME }} --os-password={{ OS_
PASSWORD }} --os-tenant-name={{ OS_TENANT_NAME }} --os-auth-url={{
OS_AUTH_URL }} aggregate-set-metadata {{ AGG_NAME }} virt_type=docker
```

The completed role and file named `main.yml` located in the `nova-scheduler/tasks`
directory looks similar to:

```
---

- name: Change default scheduler filters
shell: chdir=/bin sed -i 's/^scheduler_default_filters.*/scheduler_
default_filters = AggregateInstanceExtraSpecsFilter,RetryFilter,
AvailabilityZoneFilter,RamFilter,ComputeFilter,ImagePropertiesFilter,
ServerGroupAntiAffinityFilter,ServerGroupAffinityFilter/' /etc/nova/
nova.conf

- name: Copy Docker section file
copy: src=dockerdest=/usr/share mode=0644

- name: Insert Docker section into Nova config
shell: chdir=/usr/share cat /usr/share/docker>> /etc/nova/nova.conf
notify: restart nova-scheduler
```

The completed role and file named `main.yml` located in the `glance-update/tasks` directory resembles the following code:

```
---

- name: Add container formats to Glance API config file
  shell: chdir=/bin sed -i '/^\[DEFAULT/a container_formats=ami,ari,aki,
  bare,ovf,ova,docker' /etc/glance/glance-api.conf
  notify: restart glance-api
```

The corresponding global variable file is named `util_container` and is saved to the `group_vars/` `directory` of the complete playbook.

```
# Here are variables related to the nova-docker setup

OS_USERNAME: admin
OS_PASSWORD: passwd
OS_TENANT_NAME: admin
OS_AUTH_URL: http://172.29.236.7:35357/v2.0
FLAVOR_NAME: m1.container
FLAVOR_ID: m1dockerctr
AGG_NAME: docker
AVAIL_ZONE: docker-zone
```

Next we created the following master playbook files, all will be located in the root of the playbook directory.

The `base.yml` file will look like this:

```
---
# This playbook deploys components needed for nova-docker.

- hosts: docker_nodes
  user: root
  remote_user: root
  sudo: yes
  roles:
      - install-docker
      - nova-docker
      - nova-update
```

The `base-openstack.yml` file will look like this:

```
---
# This playbook deploys components needed for nova-docker.

- hosts: util_container
```

```
user: root
remote_user: root
sudo: yes
roles:
    - openstack-config
```

The `base-scheduler.yml` file will look like this:

```
---
# This playbook deploys components needed for nova-docker.

- hosts: nova_schedulers
user: root
remote_user: root
sudo: yes
roles:
    - nova-scheduler
```

The `base-glance.yml` file will look like this:

```
---
# This playbook deploys components needed for nova-docker.

- hosts: glance_container
user: root
remote_user: root
sudo: yes
roles:
    - glance-update
```

At the end of that we created the `hosts` file, which also is located in the root of the playbook directory.

```
[docker_nodes]
021579-docker02

[util_container]
172.29.236.179

[nova_schedulers]
172.29.236.218

[glance_container]
172.29.236.115
```

The complete set of code can again be found in the following GitHub repository: `https://github.com/os-admin-with-ansible/os-admin-with-ansible/tree/master/nova-docker`.

Now the fun part, time to test out our new playbooks and roles. There are a few more steps required to completely test this new feature. Those additional steps are outlined in the following section. Assuming that you cloned the GitHub repository earlier, the command to test out the playbook from the `Deployment` node will be as follows:

```
$ cd os-admin-with-ansible/nova-docker
$ ansible-playbook -i hosts base.yml
$ ansible-playbook -i hosts base-openstack.yml
$ ansible-playbook -i hosts base-scheduler.yml
$ ansible-playbook -i hosts base-glance.yml
```

You must now add the Docker compute node(s) to the host aggregate that was just created via the preceding roles. This can be done through the Horizon dashboard and/or via the Nova CLI. If you choose to use the CLI, the nova aggregate-add-host command will add the compute nodes to the host aggregate. The order in which they are added does not matter. As a challenge, why don't you try to add this task to the roles we just created? Do share it with us on GitHub once you do, we would love to see how you handled it.

Next, we are ready to pull a Docker image and save it directly to Glance. First, you must log into the Docker compute node(s) that you just set up. You can pull any image of your choice or use the following example:

```
$ sourceopenrc
$ docker pull busybox
$ docker save busybox | glance image-create --is-public=True \
  --container-format=docker --disk-format=raw --name busybox
```

The output from these commands will look similar to this:

```
root@021579-compute04:~# docker save busybox | glance image-create --is-public=True \
> --container-format=docker --disk-format=raw --name busybox
+------------------+--------------------------------------+
| Property         | Value                                |
+------------------+--------------------------------------+
| checksum         | 2240122d651635f5da0bc3632a0c92a3     |
| container_format | docker                               |
| created_at       | 2015-10-19T15:13:01                  |
| deleted          | False                                |
| deleted_at       | None                                 |
| disk_format      | raw                                  |
| id               | 98828714-a875-4c32-8508-c7d00111d557 |
| is_public        | True                                 |
| min_disk         | 0                                    |
| min_ram          | 0                                    |
| name             | busybox                              |
| owner            | 7ce9ae8ffa004ec19bee6fd682b8df6f     |
| protected        | False                                |
```

Now let's give it a go!

```
$ nova boot --flavor m1.container --image busybox --availability-zone
docker-zone test-ctr01
```

Check if everything went as expected:

```
$ nova list
```

You should see the instance/container running, and as a double check, execute the following Docker command and you should see your Docker container running:

```
$ dockerps
```

Congratulations, you just launched your first Docker container from within OpenStack!

Summary

Yes! You just added a new OpenStack feature to your cloud. The flexibility and gained capability due to having multiple hypervisors as a part of your cloud is huge. Have fun with your new Docker compute node(s). But before concluding this chapter, let's take a moment to recap. We talked about the benefits of multiple hypervisor support and explained why using Docker as a hypervisor within OpenStack is a good use case. Next we manually walked through the setup process for adding Docker as a compute node (Docker and nova-docker driver). Lastly, we developed the Ansible playbook and role to automate adding the OpenStack feature of using Docker as a hypervisor to your cloud

The next chapter happens to be something that came in as a customer demand for a pretty large OpenStack cloud. There is no cloud operator out there who does not want to know or have a complete inventory of their cloud. Tracking resources, auditing users, and recapping network utilization are just a few things that are a part of the daily/weekly routine for us. Imagine you can have a complete report created on one command. Possible? Well, I am not telling; you will have to read *Chapter 9, Inventory Your Cloud*, to find out.

9
Inventory Your Cloud

I am very excited to dive into this chapter, as we will focus on a topic that is considered challenging when administering an OpenStack cloud. Gathering metrics around the system being consumed is pretty high on the daily priority list. The bad news is that OpenStack does not necessarily make this an easy task. In OpenStack's defense, I will say that there has been great work done around the most recent releases to improve this. The new **OpenStackClient** (OSC) has done a good job allowing the cloud operator to pull together various metrics about the cloud.

In the mean time, there are ways to collect these metrics in an ad hoc fashion and then put a very simple report together. As with most things related to OpenStack, there are a few ways to approach it. After attempting to do this using multiple methods, I found that it was the easiest to accomplish by executing queries against the OpenStack databases. I know… no one wants to touch the database. In my past life, I used to be a DBA and one thing I learned from that experience is that simple and clearly defined queries are of no harm to any database. Combining this theory and using a tool like Ansible to pull all the information collected is a winning combo. In this chapter, we will review how you can inventory the various pieces of your OpenStack cloud resources, dynamically. We will learn which metrics are of value and how that information can be stored for later reference as well. This is an extremely powerful tool to have as a cloud operator. In this chapter, we will cover the following topics:

- Collecting cloud metrics
- User report
- Tenant report
- Network report
- Volume report
- Cloud-at-a-glance report
- Coding the playbook and roles
- Playbook and role review

Collecting cloud metrics

The first step in this process is to determine what metrics are important to you. Keep in mind that the approach outlined here is my own way of tackling this. As a cloud operator, you may have a different way in which you wish to handle this. Use this as a springboard to get you started.

From my experience, it is better to pull together user, tenant, network, and volume metrics; then take all that data, combine it together and output total cloud utilization metrics. This is very similar to what the Horizon dashboard does. While it is easy to log into Horizon and do a quick review, what if you wanted to provide a comprehensive report to your leadership? Or maybe you wanted to take a point-in-time snapshot to compare cloud utilization over a time period. There may be a possible requirement to audit your cloud one day. There exists no real easy way to do this in a report format without using a third-party tool. All of these scenarios can be satisfied using the approach outlined next.

Let's start at the beginning by taking a look at collecting user metrics first.

User report

Capturing information about the users defined in your cloud is probably the simplest metric to record. When the day comes that you have to audit your cloud for compliance and security reasons, you will notice that you list out the users and even list out the roles assigned to the users but not both of them together. Similarly, you can list out the users in a tenant but not the role assigned to that user for that tenant together. You can see where I am going with this. It makes sense to have a complete list of the users with their IDs, what roles they are assigned and to what tenant(s)/project(s) they have access to in one report. Using the following simple database query, you can very easily attain this information:

```
USE keystone;
SELECT user.id, user.name as username, user.enabled, role.name as
role, project.name as tenant from user
INNER JOIN assignment ON user.id=assignment.actor_id
INNER JOIN role ON assignment.role_id=role.id
INNER JOIN project ON assignment.target_id=project.id
ORDER BY tenant;
```

This query will combine the data from four different tables within the database called **keystone**. The keystone database is the owner of all the user related data. Each table within the database has at least one primary key that can be used to link the data together. Here is a quick breakdown of the tables used here and their functions:

```
User  # contains the raw user information such as ID, name, password
and etc.
```

```
Assignment   # contains the role assignment for all users
Role   # is the list of roles created/available
Project   # contains the list of projects/tenants created/available
```

In this example, we will focus on only pulling back the necessary columns from the four tables. To make things a bit easier to read, we also renamed a few of the column labels. Lastly, we will sort the data by the tenant name in an ascending order to give us a clean and easy output. I promise not to get too much into the weeds on this SQL query. This is a book on OpenStack and Ansible, not SQL commands, right (LOL)?

ProTip

Always try to use the ID column of the table to link data from other tables when possible. The ID column will always be a unique value that will provide reliable data correlation every time. Using columns that contain item name values might eventually cause a conflict, if a row exists in the table with duplicate values. Even OpenStack on the whole uses this approach, as you will note that anything created within OpenStack has an ID associated with it.

After executing this query, the output will look something like to the following screenshot:

```
root@infra1_galera_container-3f1f79fb:~# mysql -u root -p
Enter password:
Welcome to the MariaDB monitor.  Commands end with ; or \g.
Your MariaDB connection id is 6665
Server version: 5.5.46-MariaDB-1-trusty-wsrep-log mariadb.org binary distribution, wsrep_25.12.r4f81826

Copyright (c) 2000, 2015, Oracle, MariaDB Corporation Ab and others.

Type 'help;' or '\h' for help. Type '\c' to clear the current input statement.

MariaDB [(none)]> USE keystone;
Reading table information for completion of table and column names
You can turn off this feature to get a quicker startup with -A

Database changed
MariaDB [keystone]> SELECT user.id, user.name as username, user.enabled, role.name as role, project.name as tenant from user
    -> INNER JOIN assignment ON user.id=assignment.actor_id
    -> INNER JOIN role ON assignment.role_id=role.id
    -> INNER JOIN project ON assignment.target_id=project.id
    -> ORDER BY tenant;
+----------------------------------+----------+---------+------------------+---------+
| id                               | username | enabled | role             | tenant  |
+----------------------------------+----------+---------+------------------+---------+
| 002e637cda194a089b6db30d4b4a71f4 | cinder   |       1 | _member_         | admin   |
| d8a9537dd4dd4d09bba60a6fc63ee47b | novav3   |       1 | _member_         | admin   |
| 2445a2437d8c4ec4b3c9424ad805d4ac | s3       |       1 | _member_         | admin   |
| d94954da908640a2994f3a0f9315395b | ec2      |       1 | _member_         | admin   |
| 477bdb97725147c0a849c8c8dadf4ddd | keystone |       1 | _member_         | admin   |
| edd115a34c0f489d8f00219f53aa3e86 | glance   |       1 | _member_         | admin   |
| 77a9b53dd0ee4ab0a1cc736faed9beeb | admin    |       1 | heat_stack_owner | admin   |
| ee87737185a846f7a976dc2b90cc8ec3 | neutron  |       1 | _member_         | admin   |
| 77a9b53dd0ee4ab0a1cc736faed9beeb | admin    |       1 | _member_         | admin   |
| 83b1c316a2844becb7c276ec1a112741 | nova     |       1 | _member_         | admin   |
| a1653913d95a4a9babc31972d51a7255 | cinderv2 |       1 | _member_         | admin   |
| 77a9b53dd0ee4ab0a1cc736faed9beeb | admin    |       1 | admin            | admin   |
| 797ffb6285be4949aa0a6eda406ab6b4 | heat     |       1 | _member_         | admin   |
| 797ffb6285be4949aa0a6eda406ab6b4 | heat     |       1 | admin            | service |
| 002e637cda194a089b6db30d4b4a71f4 | cinder   |       1 | admin            | service |
| d8a9537dd4dd4d09bba60a6fc63ee47b | novav3   |       1 | admin            | service |
```

Tenant report

Having a clear view of what tenant(s)/project(s) exist within your cloud and the resources being utilized can be very valuable throughout the overall cloud life cycle. Doing department or division chargebacks seems to be a very popular approach of late and pulling these metrics as a point-in-time resources review can provide clarity around how many resources each tenant is using. To successfully accomplish this, the vCPU, memory, and disk metrics must be collected for each tenant/project. You can get this information very easily using the following simple database query:

```
USE nova;
SELECT SUM(instances.vcpus) as vCPU, SUM(instances.memory_mb) as
memory_MB, SUM(instances.root_gb) as disk_GB, keystone.project.name as
tenant from instances
INNER JOIN keystone.project ON instances.project_id=keystone.project.
id
WHERE instances.vm_state='active' GROUP BY tenant;
```

This query will combine data from two different tables that live within two separate databases, nova and keystone. The nova database is the owner of all the instance related data. The keystone database was reviewed in the prior section. Just as in the earlier example, each table has at least one primary key. Here is a quick breakdown of the tables used and their functions:

```
nova
Instances  # contains the raw information about instances created

keystone
Project  # contains the list of projects/tenants created/available
```

For attaining this data, we had to get a bit crafty and pull the resource metrics directly from the table containing the raw instance information. If we had a *Ceilometer* installed, there might have been a specific database where these metrics were recorded on a much more micro level. Since we do not have this functionality available at the time, this method is the best thing available. In this query, we will again only return the necessary columns and rename column labels. At the end, we will narrow down the output to include only active instances and sort the data by the tenant name in ascending order. So, by pulling the resource information about each instance and correlating it to each tenant where the instance belongs, we can create a simple output similar to the following example:

```
root@infra1_galera_container-3f1f79fb:~# mysql -u root -p
Enter password:
Welcome to the MariaDB monitor.  Commands end with ; or \g.
Your MariaDB connection id is 6704
Server version: 5.5.46-MariaDB-1-trusty-wsrep-log mariodb.org binary distribution, wsrep_25.12.r4f81026

Copyright (c) 2000, 2015, Oracle, MariaDB Corporation Ab and others.

Type 'help;' or '\h' for help. Type '\c' to clear the current input statement.

MariaDB [(none)]> USE nova;
Reading table information for completion of table and column names
You can turn off this feature to get a quicker startup with -A

Database changed
MariaDB [nova]> SELECT SUM(instances.vcpus) as vCPU, SUM(instances.memory_mb) as memory_MB, SUM(instances.root_gb)
    -> INNER JOIN keystone.project ON instances.project_id=keystone.project.id
    -> WHERE instances.vm_state='active' GROUP BY tenant;
+------+-----------+---------+---------+
| vCPU | memory_MB | disk_GB | tenant  |
+------+-----------+---------+---------+
|    4 |      2048 |       4 | admin   |
|    2 |      4096 |      40 | tenantA |
|    5 |      5632 |      43 | tenantB |
+------+-----------+---------+---------+
3 rows in set (0.03 sec)
```

Network report

While having network metrics is not as critical to managing your overall OpenStack cloud, it is useful information to have. Unnecessary or incorrectly configured networks can add latency to the overall cloud functionality. It is not the network directly that might cause this but rather the security groups related to each tenant(s)/project(s) existing network. This information can mainly aid in troubleshooting tenant reported issues. It provides a quick reference about what networks exist within what tenant and the network **CIDR (Classless Inter-Domain Routing** aka network address space) associated. Natively, the networking service (Neutron) within one command does not provide such a report. Just as earlier, we will pull this information directly from the database. Using the following simple database query, we will collect the network ID, name, subnet, CIDR assigned, status, and associated tenant:

```
USE neutron;
SELECT networks.id, networks.name, subnets.name as subnet, subnets.
cidr, networks.status, networks.shared, keystone.project.name as
tenant from networks
INNER JOIN keystone.project ON networks.tenant_id COLLATE utf8_
unicode_ci = keystone.project.id
INNER JOIN subnets ON networks.id=subnets.network_id
ORDER BY tenant;
```

For this query, we will combine data from three different tables that live within two separate databases, neutron and keystone. The neutron database is the owner of all the network related data. Here is a quick breakdown of the tables used here and their functions:

```
neutron
Networks  # contains the raw information about networks created
Subnets   # contains the subnet details associated with the networks

keystone
Project   # contains the list of projects/tenants created/available
```

Collecting these metrics was rather straightforward because most of the data existed within the networks table. All we had to do is pull in the matching CIDR taken from the subnet table and then bring in the tenant name associated with that network. While putting this query together, I noticed that there was an issue joining the keystone and neutron database tables. Apparently, the neutron database defined the schema for the ID column differently and the following value had to be added to the inner join statement: COLLATE utf8_unicode_ci. At the end, the output will be sorted by the tenant names in ascending order. An example of the output will look similar to the following screenshot:

```
root@infra1_galera_container-3f1f79fb:~# mysql -u root -p
Enter password:
Welcome to the MariaDB monitor.  Commands end with ; or \g.
Your MariaDB connection id is 6710
Server version: 5.5.46-MariaDB-1-trusty-wsrep-log mariadb.org binary distribution, wsrep_25.12.r4f81826

Copyright (c) 2000, 2015, Oracle, MariaDB Corporation Ab and others.

Type 'help;' or '\h' for help. Type '\c' to clear the current input statement.

MariaDB [(none)]> USE neutron;
Reading table information for completion of table and column names
You can turn off this feature to get a quicker startup with -A

Database changed
MariaDB [neutron]> SELECT networks.id, networks.name, subnets.name as subnet, subnets.cidr, networks.status, networks.shared, keysto
    -> INNER JOIN keystone.project ON networks.tenant_id COLLATE utf8_unicode_ci = keystone.project.id
    -> INNER JOIN subnets ON networks.id=subnets.network_id
    -> ORDER BY tenant;
+--------------------------------------+-----------------+------------------------+----------------+----------+--------+--------+
| id                                   | name            | subnet                 | cidr           | status   | shared | tenant |
+--------------------------------------+-----------------+------------------------+----------------+----------+--------+--------+
| 575b1f4c-fe6e-40d7-9b18-c673ad13ce4b | private-network | subnet-private-network | 10.1.100.0/24  | ACTIVE   |      1 | admin  |
+--------------------------------------+-----------------+------------------------+----------------+----------+--------+--------+
1 row in set (0.00 sec)
```

Volume report

The capability to have detailed reports on the overall volume consumption within the cloud seems to be a rather big gap within OpenStack. The block storage service (Cinder) is responsible for maintaining and tracking the volumes within the cloud. To get accurate metrics, we need to query Cinder directly. It would be nice to have a report to breakdown the volumes created and organized by tenant/project. Then be able to have a quick roll-up report to show how much volume storage each tenant/project is using. Now, since Cinder supports multiple storage backends, it would be best for you to keep track of the volume type consumption as well. As Cinder matures, I am sure this will become an easier task, but for now we can again query the database directly to pull out the metrics we are seeking. The following are the examples of the database queries that are used to collect these metrics:

```
USE cinder;
SELECT volumes.id, volumes.display_name as volume_name, volumes.size
as size_GB, volume_types.name as volume_type, keystone.project.name as
tenant from volumes
INNER JOIN keystone.project ON volumes.project_id=keystone.project.id
INNER JOIN volume_types ON volumes.volume_type_id=volume_types.id
WHERE volumes.status='available'
ORDER BY tenant;

SELECT SUM(volumes.size) as volume_usage_GB, keystone.project.name as
tenant from volumes
INNER JOIN keystone.project ON volumes.project_id=keystone.project.id
WHERE volumes.status='available'
GROUP BY tenant;

SELECT volume_types.name as volume_type, SUM(volumes.size) as volume_
usage_GB from volumes
INNER JOIN volume_types ON volumes.volume_type_id=volume_types.id
WHERE volumes.status='available'
GROUP BY volume_type;
```

For this query, at least three separate tables were involved and it included two databases: `cinder` and `keystone`. It requires us to issue three separate SELECT statements. The first SELECT statement will correlate the raw volume information from the `volumes` table with the tenant/project data from the `keystone` table. Also, we will include the name of the volume type within this same statement. Since the `volumes` table contains both active and inactive volumes there has to be an additional filter applied to return only the active volumes. The complete output will then be sorted by the tenant name in ascending order. An example of the output will look similar to the following screenshot:

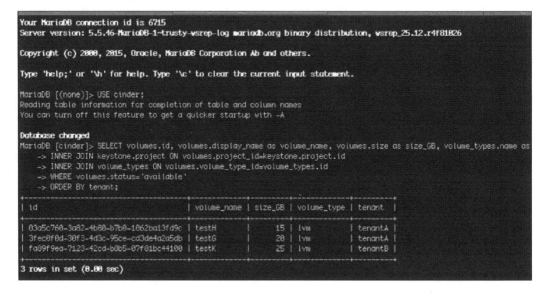

The next SELECT statement will query the database to collect the metrics for the total volume consumption per tenant/project. It is very similar to the previous statement, but the main difference here is that we are going to add the `volume_usage_GB` column together for each tenant/project to calculate the total consumption amounts. An example of the output will look similar to the following screenshot:

```
MariaDB [cinder]>
MariaDB [cinder]> SELECT SUM(volumes.size) as volume_usage_GB, keystone.project.name as tenant from volumes
    -> INNER JOIN keystone.project ON volumes.project_id=keystone.project.id
    -> WHERE volumes.status='available'
    -> GROUP BY tenant;
+-----------------+---------+
| volume_usage_GB | tenant  |
+-----------------+---------+
|              35 | tenantA |
|              25 | tenantB |
+-----------------+---------+
2 rows in set (0.00 sec)
```

The final SELECT statement focuses on reporting the volume type consumption. Since the volumes table only records the volume type ID, we had to inner join the volume_types table to pull in the actual volume name defined when created. This was something that was also done for the other statements. An example of the output will look similar to the following screenshot:

```
MariaDB [cinder]>
MariaDB [cinder]> SELECT volume_types.name as volume_type, SUM(volumes.size) as volume_usage_GB from volumes
    -> INNER JOIN volume_types ON volumes.volume_type_id=volume_types.id
    -> WHERE volumes.status='available'
    -> GROUP BY volume_type;
+-------------+-----------------+
| volume_type | volume_usage_GB |
+-------------+-----------------+
| lvm         |              60 |
+-------------+-----------------+
1 row in set (0.01 sec)
```

Cloud-at-a-glance report

This report is meant to be a very quick snapshot of the cloud's overall consumption. It pulls back the total number of users, tenants, volumes, and networks existing within your cloud. As well as, the total number of vCPU, memory, and ephemeral disk currently utilized. The following are the database queries that are used to collect this data:

```
USE keystone;
SELECT count(*) as total_users from user
WHERE user.enabled=1;

SELECT count(*) as total_tenants from project
WHERE project.enabled=1;

USE cinder;
SELECT count(*) as total_volumes, SUM(volumes.size) as total_volume_
usage_GB from volumes
WHERE volumes.status='available';

USE neutron;
SELECT count(*) as total_networks from networks
WHERE networks.status='ACTIVE';

USE nova;
SELECT SUM(instances.vcpus) as total_vCPU, SUM(instances.memory_mb)
as total_memory_MB, SUM(instances.root_gb) as total_disk_GB from
instances
WHERE instances.vm_state='active';
```

The SELECT statements used basically add together the columns from the table being called. The column is then renamed to a more descriptive label and finally filtered to ignore any rows that are not in an active state. Once executed, the output of the above queries will look similar to the following screenshot:

```
MariaDB [(none)]> USE keystone;
Reading table information for completion of table and column names
You can turn off this feature to get a quicker startup with -A

Database changed
MariaDB [keystone]> SELECT count(*) as total_users from user
    -> WHERE user.enabled=1;
+-------------+
| total_users |
+-------------+
|          14 |
+-------------+
1 row in set (0.00 sec)

MariaDB [keystone]>
MariaDB [keystone]> SELECT count(*) as total_tenants from project
    -> WHERE project.enabled=1;
+---------------+
| total_tenants |
+---------------+
|             4 |
+---------------+
1 row in set (0.00 sec)

MariaDB [keystone]>
MariaDB [keystone]> USE cinder;
Reading table information for completion of table and column names
You can turn off this feature to get a quicker startup with -A

Database changed
MariaDB [cinder]> SELECT count(*) as total_volumes, SUM(volumes.size) as total_volume_usage_GB from volumes
    -> WHERE volumes.status='available';
+---------------+-----------------------+
| total_volumes | total_volume_usage_GB |
+---------------+-----------------------+
|             3 |                    60 |
+---------------+-----------------------+
1 row in set (0.00 sec)

MariaDB [cinder]>
MariaDB [cinder]> USE neutron;
Reading table information for completion of table and column names
You can turn off this feature to get a quicker startup with -A

Database changed
MariaDB [neutron]> SELECT count(*) as total_networks from networks
    -> WHERE networks.status='ACTIVE';
+----------------+
| total_networks |
+----------------+
|              1 |
+----------------+
1 row in set (0.00 sec)

MariaDB [neutron]>
MariaDB [neutron]> USE nova;
Reading table information for completion of table and column names
You can turn off this feature to get a quicker startup with -A

Database changed
MariaDB [nova]> SELECT SUM(instances.vcpus) as total_vCPU, SUM(instances.memory_mb) as total_memory_MB, SUM(instances.root_gb) as total_d
    -> WHERE instances.vm_state='active';
+------------+-----------------+---------------+
| total_vCPU | total_memory_MB | total_disk_GB |
+------------+-----------------+---------------+
|         11 |           11776 |            87 |
+------------+-----------------+---------------+
1 row in set (0.00 sec)
```

Now that we know how to collect the metrics for our reports, let's go and learn how we can automate this task completely.

Coding the playbook and roles

In this section, we will create the playbook and its role is to generate a comprehensive *cloud report*. Once the playbook is executed, the output and end result will be two separate reports consisting of the information we learned in the previous section. These two reports will be saved in a directory determined by you for retrieval. At this point, you can literally send it to leadership and/or peers for review. In the next chapter, we will learn how you can take things further and directly email the report as an added bonus.

Very similar to the last chapter, we will break up the multiple tasks into separate roles to keep things organized. We will now review the six roles used to automate creating our *cloud report*.

cloud-inventory

The first role that we will create will include the tasks needed to set up the foundation for the cloud report. The name of the file will be `main.yml` located within the role directory named `cloud-inventory/tasks`. The contents of this file will look similar to the following code block:

```
---
- name: Create working directory
  shell: mkdir {{ REPORT_DIR }}
  ignore_errors: yes

- name: Copy the cloud_report script
  copy: src=cloud_report.sqldest=/usr/share mode=0755

- name: Add report header
  shell: ( echo "+----------------------------------------+"; echo "|
  {{ COMPANY }} Cloud Report              |"; echo "| Created at {{
  lookup('pipe', 'date +%Y-%m-%d%t%X') }}   |"; echo "+-----------
  ------------------------+"; ) >> {{ REPORT_DIR }}/os_report_{{
  lookup('pipe', 'date +%Y%m%d') }}.log

- name: Execute cloud report
  shell: chdir=/usr/bin mysql -u root --password={{ MYSQLPASS }}
  --table < /usr/share/cloud_report.sql>> {{ REPORT_DIR }}/os_report_{{
  lookup('pipe', 'date +%Y%m%d') }}.log
```

The first three tasks simply handle the prerequisite steps needed to create the report. This will include creating the directory where the report is to be saved, copying the SQL script to be executed, and adding the header to the report. The overall idea is to create a visually appealing, accurate, and flexible report. One way this can be accomplished is by adding the report run time/date dynamically and naming the report accordingly. The final task will execute the `cloud_report.sql` file directly against the MySQL database found in the Galera container of your cloud.

The `cloud_report.sql` file contains the SQL query described in the preceding *Cloud-at-a-glance report* section. This file can be found within the `cloud-inventory/files` directory of this role.

cloud-usage

The next role in the line up will create the second report that will outline the current cloud utilization broken down per tenant/project. The file will be named `main.yml` and will be located within the role directory name `cloud-usage/tasks`. The contents of this file will look similar to the following code block:

```
---
- name: Create working directory
  shell: mkdir {{ REPORT_DIR }}
  ignore_errors: yes


- name: Retrieve tenantIDs
  shell: keystone --os-username={{ OS_USERNAME }} --os-password={{ OS_
  PASSWORD }} --os-tenant-name={{ OS_TENANT_NAME }} --os-auth-url={{
  OS_AUTH_URL }}
  tenant-list | awk 'NR > 3 { print $2 }'
  register: tenantid


- name: Add report header
  shell: ( echo "+------------------------------------+"; echo "| Tenant
  Usage Report                 |"; echo "| Created at {{ lookup('pipe',
  'date +%Y-%m-%d%t%X') }}  |"; echo "+-------------------------
  -----------+"; echo ""; ) >> {{ REPORT_DIR }}/os_usage_report_{{
  lookup('pipe', 'date +%Y%m%d') }}.log


- name: Record tenant usage
  shell: ( echo "Tenant - {{ item }}"&& nova --os-username={{ OS_
  USERNAME }} --os-password={{ OS_PASSWORD }} --os-tenant-name={{ OS_
  TENANT_NAME }} --os-auth-url={{ OS_AUTH_URL }}
  usage --start {{ RPTSTART }} --end {{ RPTEND }} --tenant {{ item }} &&
  echo "" ) >> {{ REPORT_DIR }}/os_usage_report_{{ lookup('pipe', 'date
  +%Y%m%d') }}.log
```

```
with_items: tenantid.stdout_lines

- name: Retrieve tenant usage report file
  fetch: src={{ REPORT_DIR }}/os_usage_report_{{ lookup('pipe', 'date
  +%Y%m%d') }}.log dest={{ REPORT_DEST }} flat=yes
```

All the pre-setup work for the report is being handled in the first and third task shown in the preceding example (creating the report directory and header). To gather the metrics that we need for this report, we can use native OpenStack CLI commands. The two commands used are: `keystone tenant-list` and `nova usage`. These commands are executed as a part of the second and fourth tasks shown earlier. The last task in this role will retrieve the report from the remote location and move it locally to where the playbook/roles are executed.

user-inventory

This role will be responsible for executing the **user report** described in the earlier section. The file will be named `main.yml` within the role directory named `user-inventory/tasks`. In the following section, you will find the contents of this file:

```
---
- name: Create working directory
  shell: mkdir {{ REPORT_DIR }}
  ignore_errors: yes

- name: Copy the user_report script
  copy: src=user_report.sqldest=/usr/share mode=0755

- name: Add report header
  shell: ( echo "+------------------------+"; echo "| Cloud User Report
  |"; echo "+------------------------+"; ) >> {{ REPORT_DIR }}/os_
  report_{{ lookup('pipe', 'date +%Y%m%d') }}.log

- name: Execute user report
  shell: chdir=/usr/bin mysql -u root --password={{ MYSQLPASS }}
  --table < /usr/share/user_report.sql>> {{ REPORT_DIR }}/os_report_{{
  lookup('pipe', 'date +%Y%m%d') }}.log
```

In an attempt to make the reports modular and not dependent on each other, I had each role create a report-working directory and insert report-specific headers. This way you can include or exclude whichever roles/reports you wish.

The basic principle used to create this role will be repeated for the remaining roles. It consists of the following steps:

1. Create the report working directory; if the directory already exists, it will continue reporting no errors.

2. Copy the SQL script to the remote location.

3. Add custom header information to the report.

4. Execute the SQL script to generate the specific sub-report.

The user_report.sql file contains the SQL query described in the preceding *User report* section. Now that we have the framework defined, we can move quickly to the remaining roles.

tenant-inventory

The purpose of this role is to execute the **tenant report** we reviewed in the earlier section. The file will be named main.yml within the role directory named tenant-inventory/tasks. In the following section, you will find the contents of this file:

```
---
- name: Create working directory
shell: mkdir {{ REPORT_DIR }}
ignore_errors: yes

- name: Copy the tenant_report script
copy: src=tenant_report.sqldest=/usr/share mode=0755

- name: Add report header
shell: ( echo "+--------------------------+"; echo "| Cloud Tenant
Report     |"; echo "+--------------------------+"; ) >> {{ REPORT_DIR
}}/os_report_{{ lookup('pipe', 'date +%Y%m%d') }}.log

- name: Execute tenant report
shell: chdir=/usr/bin mysql -u root --password={{ MYSQLPASS }}
--table < /usr/share/tenant_report.sql>> {{ REPORT_DIR }}/os_report_{{
lookup('pipe', 'date +%Y%m%d') }}.log
```

Since this role will follow the same steps outlined for the user-inventory role, we will draw attention to the unique function executed. For this role, the tenant_report.sql file will contain the SQL query described in the preceding *Tenant report* section.

network-inventory

The purpose of this role is to execute the **network report**, which we reviewed in the earlier section. The file will be named `main.yml` within the role directory named `network-inventory/tasks`. In the following example, you will find the contents of this file:

```
---
- name: Create working directory
  shell: mkdir {{ REPORT_DIR }}
  ignore_errors: yes

- name: Copy the network_report script
  copy: src=network_report.sqldest=/usr/share mode=0755

- name: Add report header
  shell: ( echo "+------------------------+"; echo "| Cloud Network
Report     |"; echo "+------------------------+"; ) >> {{ REPORT_DIR
}}/os_report_{{ lookup('pipe', 'date +%Y%m%d') }}.log

- name: Execute network report
  shell: chdir=/usr/bin mysql -u root --password={{ MYSQLPASS }} --table
< /usr/share/network_report.sql>> {{ REPORT_DIR }}/os_report_{{
lookup('pipe', 'date +%Y%m%d') }}.log
```

volume-inventory

This last role will execute the final sub-report, which is the **volume report** we covered earlier. The file will be named `main.yml` within the role directory named `volume-inventory/tasks`. In the following example, you will find the contents of this file:

```
---
- name: Create working directory
  shell: mkdir {{ REPORT_DIR }}
  ignore_errors: yes

- name: Copy the volume_report script
  copy: src=volume_report.sqldest=/usr/share mode=0755

- name: Add report header
  shell: ( echo "+--------------------------+"; echo "| Cloud Volume
Report     |"; echo "+--------------------------+"; ) >> {{ REPORT_
DIR }}/os_report_{{ lookup('pipe', 'date +%Y%m%d') }}.log
```

```
- name: Execute volume report
shell: chdir=/usr/bin mysql -u root --password={{ MYSQLPASS }}
--table < /usr/share/volume_report.sql>> {{ REPORT_DIR }}/os_report_{{
lookup('pipe', 'date +%Y%m%d') }}.log

- name: Retrieve completed cloud report file
fetch: src={{ REPORT_DIR }}/os_report_{{ lookup('pipe', 'date
+%Y%m%d') }}.log dest={{ REPORT_DEST }} flat=yes
```

One special thing worth noting about this role is that the last task uses the `fetch` Ansible module to retrieve the report created from the remote location where it was created. This same behavior is used in the cloud-usage role. Personally, I thought this module was very convenient and kept us from having to handle a series of secure copy commands; it is never a good time for anyone.

To support these roles we need to create the variable files that will go along with them. Since we will use two separate hosts to execute the series of roles against, there will be two global variable files needed. The file names are `util_container` and `galera_container`, they will be saved to the `group_vars/` directory of the playbook.

 Note that the values defined in the variable file are intended to be changed before each execution for normal everyday use.

You will notice a few new variables that were defined for the new roles. Among the standard variables needed to authenticate into your OpenStack cloud, we have added some new variables related to the report creation and location:

```
util_container

# Here are variables related globally to the util_container host group

OS_USERNAME: ansible
OS_PASSWORD: passwd
OS_TENANT_NAME: admin
OS_AUTH_URL: http://172.29.236.7:35357/v2.0
OS_SERVICE_TOKEN: passwd
REPORT_DIR: /usr/share/os-report
REPORT_DEST: /usr/share/
RPTSTART: 2015-09-01
RPTEND: 2015-10-03


galera_container
```

```
# Here are variables related globally to the galera_container host
group

MYSQLPASS: passwd
COMPANY: Rackspace RPC
REPORT_DIR: /usr/share/os-report
REPORT_DEST: /usr/share/
```

A word of caution

Due to the contents of this file, it should be stored as a secure file within whatever code repository you may use to store your Ansible playbooks/ roles. Gaining access to this information will compromise your OpenStack cloud security.

Let's take a moment to break down the new variables. The summary will be:

```
REPORT_DIR  # the directory where the report is stored temporarily
remotely

REPORT_DEST  # the directory where the report is saved locally

RPTSTART  # the start date when collecting cloud usage

RPTEND    # the end date when collecting cloud usage

MYSQLPASS # the password for the root database user

COMPANY   # the company name to show up in the report header
```

Since there are two global variable files that share the same variable names, make sure to keep the variable value in sync if you want both reports in the same directory. This is not a requirement, as each report (*cloud report* and *cloud usage*) can exist independently. I just felt like it was worth mentioning, so as to avoid confusion.

With the variable file completed, we can move on to creating the master playbook file. Since our goal is to create a report on the cloud resources (remember we added the cloud usage report as a bonus) we will call all the roles from one playbook. The complete contents of the playbook file will end up looking similar to this:

```
---
# This playbook used to run a cloud resource inventory report.

- hosts: galera_container
  user: root
  remote_user: root
  sudo: yes
  roles:
  - cloud-inventory

- hosts: util_container
  user: root
  remote_user: root
  sudo: yes
  roles:
  - cloud-usage

- hosts: galera_container
  user: root
  remote_user: root
  sudo: yes
  roles:
  - user-inventory
  - tenant-inventory
  - network-inventory
  - volume-inventory
```

As mentioned, all the roles we created to inventory the cloud will be executed in the order displayed in the playbook. All the roles utilize the same host with the exception of the `cloud-usage` role. The reason behind this is that we used the OpenStack CLI command in that role and that then needed the use of the `util_container`.

> The playbook and role names can be anything you choose. Specific names have been provided here in order to allow you to easily follow along and reference the completed code found in the GitHub repository. The only warning is whatever you decide to name the roles; it must remain uniform when referenced from within the playbook(s).

So, since we now have one additional host involved in this playbook, we must add this host to our inventory file. With the addition of the new host placeholder, the host file will now look similar to the following example:

```
[localhost]
localhostansible_connection=local

[util_container]
172.29.236.85

[galera_container]
172.29.236.72
```

I am extremely excited to confirm that we are now ready to start running some cloud reports. In keeping with our tradition, we will finish up the chapter with a quick review of the playbook and role just created.

Playbook and role review

Let's jump right into examining the roles we created.

The completed role and file named `main.yml` located in the `cloud-inventory/tasks` directory looks similar to this:

```
---
- name: Create working directory
  shell: mkdir {{ REPORT_DIR }}
  ignore_errors: yes

- name: Copy the cloud_report script
  copy: src=cloud_report.sqldest=/usr/share mode=0755

- name: Add report header
  shell: ( echo "+------------------------------------+"; echo "|
{{ COMPANY }} Cloud Report           |"; echo "| Created at {{
lookup('pipe', 'date +%Y-%m-%d%t%X') }}  |"; echo "+-----------
------------------------+"; ) >> {{ REPORT_DIR }}/os_report_{{
lookup('pipe', 'date +%Y%m%d') }}.log

- name: Execute cloud report
  shell: chdir=/usr/bin mysql -u root --password={{ MYSQLPASS }}
--table < /usr/share/cloud_report.sql>> {{ REPORT_DIR }}/os_report_{{
lookup('pipe', 'date +%Y%m%d') }}.log
```

The completed role and file named `main.yml` located in the `cloud-usage/tasks`
directory looks similar to this:

```
---
- name: Create working directory
  shell: mkdir {{ REPORT_DIR }}
  ignore_errors: yes

- name: Retrieve tenantIDs
  shell: keystone --os-username={{ OS_USERNAME }} --os-password={{ OS_
    PASSWORD }} --os-tenant-name={{ OS_TENANT_NAME }} --os-auth-url={{
    OS_AUTH_URL }}
    tenant-list | awk 'NR > 3 { print $2 }'
  register: tenantid

- name: Add report header
  shell: ( echo "+------------------------------------+"; echo "| Tenant
    Usage Report                |"; echo "| Created at {{ lookup('pipe',
    'date +%Y-%m-%d%t%X') }}  |"; echo "+-------------------------
    ----------+"; echo ""; ) >> {{ REPORT_DIR }}/os_usage_report_{{
    lookup('pipe', 'date +%Y%m%d') }}.log

- name: Record tenant usage
  shell: ( echo "Tenant - {{ item }}"&& nova --os-username={{ OS_
    USERNAME }} --os-password={{ OS_PASSWORD }} --os-tenant-name={{ OS_
    TENANT_NAME }} --os-auth-url={{ OS_AUTH_URL }}
    usage --start {{ RPTSTART }} --end {{ RPTEND }} --tenant {{ item }} &&
    echo "" ) >> {{ REPORT_DIR }}/os_usage_report_{{ lookup('pipe', 'date
    +%Y%m%d') }}.log
  with_items: tenantid.stdout_lines

- name: Retrieve tenant usage report file
  fetch: src={{ REPORT_DIR }}/os_usage_report_{{ lookup('pipe', 'date
    +%Y%m%d') }}.log dest={{ REPORT_DEST }} flat=yes
```

The completed role and file named `main.yml` located in the `user-inventory/tasks`
directory looks similar to this:

```
---
- name: Create working directory
  shell: mkdir {{ REPORT_DIR }}
  ignore_errors: yes

- name: Copy the user_report script
  copy: src=user_report.sqldest=/usr/share mode=0755
```

```
- name: Add report header
  shell: ( echo "+------------------------+"; echo "| Cloud User Report
  |"; echo "+------------------------+"; ) >> {{ REPORT_DIR }}/os_
  report_{{ lookup('pipe', 'date +%Y%m%d') }}.log

- name: Execute user report
  shell: chdir=/usr/bin mysql -u root --password={{ MYSQLPASS }}
  --table < /usr/share/user_report.sql>> {{ REPORT_DIR }}/os_report_{{
  lookup('pipe', 'date +%Y%m%d') }}.log
```

The completed role and file named `main.yml` located in the `tenant-inventory/` `tasks` directory looks similar to this:

```
---
- name: Create working directory
  shell: mkdir {{ REPORT_DIR }}
  ignore_errors: yes

- name: Copy the tenant_report script
  copy: src=tenant_report.sqldest=/usr/share mode=0755

- name: Add report header
  shell: ( echo "+-------------------------+"; echo "| Cloud Tenant
  Report     |"; echo "+-------------------------+"; ) >> {{ REPORT_DIR
  }}/os_report_{{ lookup('pipe', 'date +%Y%m%d') }}.log

- name: Execute tenant report
  shell: chdir=/usr/bin mysql -u root --password={{ MYSQLPASS }}
  --table < /usr/share/tenant_report.sql>> {{ REPORT_DIR }}/os_report_{{
  lookup('pipe', 'date +%Y%m%d') }}.log
```

The completed role and file named `main.yml` located in the `network-inventory/` `tasks` directory looks similar to this:

```
---
- name: Create working directory
  shell: mkdir {{ REPORT_DIR }}
  ignore_errors: yes

- name: Copy the network_report script
  copy: src=network_report.sqldest=/usr/share mode=0755

- name: Add report header
  shell: ( echo "+-------------------------+"; echo "| Cloud Network
  Report     |"; echo "+-------------------------+"; ) >> {{ REPORT_DIR
  }}/os_report_{{ lookup('pipe', 'date +%Y%m%d') }}.log
```

```
- name: Execute network report
shell: chdir=/usr/bin mysql -u root --password={{ MYSQLPASS }} --table
< /usr/share/network_report.sql>> {{ REPORT_DIR }}/os_report_{{
lookup('pipe', 'date +%Y%m%d') }}.log
```

The completed role and file named `main.yml` located in the `volume-inventory/` `tasks` directory looks similar to this:

```
---
- name: Create working directory
shell: mkdir {{ REPORT_DIR }}
ignore_errors: yes

- name: Copy the volume_report script
copy: src=volume_report.sqldest=/usr/share mode=0755

- name: Add report header
shell: ( echo "+--------------------------+"; echo "| Cloud Volume
Report      |"; echo "+--------------------------+"; ) >> {{ REPORT_
DIR }}/os_report_{{ lookup('pipe', 'date +%Y%m%d') }}.log

- name: Execute volume report
shell: chdir=/usr/bin mysql -u root --password={{ MYSQLPASS }}
--table < /usr/share/volume_report.sql>> {{ REPORT_DIR }}/os_report_{{
lookup('pipe', 'date +%Y%m%d') }}.log

- name: Retrieve completed cloud report file
fetch: src={{ REPORT_DIR }}/os_report_{{ lookup('pipe', 'date
+%Y%m%d') }}.log dest={{ REPORT_DEST }} flat=yes
```

The corresponding global variable file is named `util_container` and is saved to the `group_vars/` directory of the complete playbook:

```
# Here are variables related globally to the util_container host group

OS_USERNAME: admin
OS_PASSWORD: passwd
OS_TENANT_NAME: admin
OS_AUTH_URL: http://172.29.236.7:35357/v2.0
REPORT_DIR: /usr/share/os-report
REPORT_DEST: /usr/share/
RPTSTART: 2015-09-01
RPTEND: 2015-10-03
```

The corresponding global variable file is named `galera_container` and is saved to the `group_vars/` directory of the complete playbook:

```
# Here are variables related globally to the galera_container host
group

MYSQLPASS: passwd
COMPANY: Rackspace RPC
REPORT_DIR: /usr/share/os-report
REPORT_DEST: /usr/share/
```

Now, the master playbook file is created and will be located in the root of the playbook directory.

The `inventory.yml` file will look as follows:

```
---
# This playbook used to run a cloud resource inventory report.

- hosts: galera_container
  user: root
  remote_user: root
  sudo: yes
  roles:
  - cloud-inventory

- hosts: util_container
  user: root
  remote_user: root
  sudo: yes
  roles:
  - cloud-usage

- hosts: galera_container
  user: root
  remote_user: root
  sudo: yes
  roles:
  - user-inventory
  - tenant-inventory
  - network-inventory
  - volume-inventory
```

Finally, at the end we created the `hosts` file, which is also located in the root of the playbook directory:

```
[localhost]
localhostansible_connection=local

[util_container]
172.29.236.85

[galera_container]
172.29.236.72
```

The complete set of code can again be found in the following GitHub repository: `https://github.com/os-admin-with-ansible/os-admin-with-ansible/tree/master/cloud-inventory`.

Before we finish this topic, we need to test our work. At the end of running this playbook and role, you will have two reports to review. Assuming that you have cloned the GitHub repository in the preceding section, the command to test out the playbook from the `Deployment` node will be as follows:

```
$ cd os-admin-with-ansible/cloud-inventory
$ ansible-playbook –i hosts inventory.yml
```

Assuming that the playbook ran successfully and completed with no errors, you should find the two reports created in the directory you specified in the global variable file. The first report should then look similar to the following screenshot:

The second report will look similar to the following screenshot shown below:

```
+-----------------------------+
| Cloud Tenant Report         |
+-----------------------------+
+------+--------+------+---------+
| vCPU | memory | disk | tenant  |
+------+--------+------+---------+
|    1 |    512 |    1 | admin   |
|    3 |   1536 |    3 | tenantA |
|    5 |   2560 |    5 | tenantB |
+------+--------+------+---------+

+-----------------------------+
| Cloud Network Report        |
+-----------------------------+
+--------------------------------------+--------+------------------+-----------------+---------------+
| id                                   |        | name             | subnet          | cidr          |
| status | shared | tenant |           |        |                  |                 |               |
+--------------------------------------+--------+------------------+-----------------+---------------+
| f3ee392c-51a1-43b3-9260-6b3c9288b052 |        | private-network  | subnet-private  | 10.1.100.0/24 |
| ACTIVE |      1 | admin  |           |        |                  |                 |               |
+--------------------------------------+--------+------------------+-----------------+---------------+

+-----------------------------+
| Cloud Volume Report         |
+-----------------------------+
+--------------------------------------+-------------+------+-------------+---------+
| id                                   | volume_name | size | volume_type | tenant  |
+--------------------------------------+-------------+------+-------------+---------+
| cf536210-85f8-4018-bb6e-6733fa296237 | testW       |   10 | lvm         | admin   |
| 1c1b6ecd-2c39-4afc-a1e2-41ef29448e07 | testY       |    2 | lvm         | tenantA |
| a6a6793f-85fe-4ba6-813f-90500869373e | testR       |    8 | lvm         | tenantA |
+--------------------------------------+-------------+------+-------------+---------+

+--------------+---------+
| volume_usage | tenant  |
+--------------+---------+
|           10 | admin   |
|           10 | tenantA |
+--------------+---------+

+-------------+--------------+
| volume_type | volume_usage |
+-------------+--------------+
| lvm         |           20 |
+-------------+--------------+
```

Job well done yet again! I am hoping that these cloud reports can really help in simplifying your day-to-day OpenStack administrative tasks!

Summary

OK, so you have just been awarded with yet another powerful tool for your OpenStack administration toolbox. Being able to generate such reports by just executing one command is pretty cool, if I must admit it myself. Just like with all the other chapters, feel free to improve the roles created here. The only thing I ask of you is to share it with everyone else when possible. Before concluding this chapter, let's take a moment to recap this chapter. Together we reviewed some gaps in OpenStack regarding reports on the cloud inventory and how you can overcome them. Then details were provided on how you can access all these great metrics/stats directly from the OpenStack database. Next, we broke down and examined the SQL queries that are used to pull out the data from the database in detail. Lastly, we developed an Ansible playbook and role to automate generating the cloud reports.

It saddens me a bit to say that the next chapter is our last chapter. With that said, it most certainly happens to probably be one of the most important chapters. Knowing the health of your cloud is tantamount to having a working OpenStack ecosystem. Due to the modular nature of OpenStack, you will have many services to keep track of. Having them all working properly is what creates the great harmony within OpenStack. While you can certainly do it manually, I am sure you will agree that automating such a task is much more ideal. Please read the next chapter to learn how to monitor the health of your cloud automatically and even have a health report delivered right to your inbox.

10
Health Check Your Cloud

The topic of monitoring happens to be something I hold very close to my heart. I have spent years 'watching' many organizations, websites, and applications to ensure that their availability holds as close as possible to 99.99% uptime. This task was not for the meek of heart in any realm of things. The thing that got me through it all was having a solid method to monitor the environments, which did not require me to literally watch them every second of the day. In this chapter, we will go through some of the most common approaches to check the health of your OpenStack cloud.

Since we have been experimenting with the **OpenStack Ansible (OSA)** deployment method throughout the book, let's continue to leverage the built-in Ansible capabilities part of OSA to perform various system checks. Remember, what we do here should not replace any third-party monitoring tool that most likely will do a better job at keeping the tasks to be monitored in a reliable rotation. We will use the native capabilities part of OpenStack and Linux to provide a quick view of your cloud's health. This quick view can then be e-mailed to you in any interval that works best for you; along the way, we will also review other monitoring tips and tricks. In this chapter, we will cover the following topics:

- Monitoring the cloud
- Infrastructure services
- Core OpenStack services
- Coding the playbook and roles
- Playbook and role review

Monitoring the cloud

I will cover some monitoring basics before getting started here. Hopefully, the three principles that I will share here are not new to you. When evaluating to monitor something, there are three base principles that you should keep in mind, they are:

- Keep it simple
- Keep your monitoring close to your infrastructure
- Create good monitors

The first point is very easy to understand, as it is rather self-explanatory. The worst thing you could ever do is over complicate something as important as monitoring. This principle not only applies to your overall approach but it also applies to the tool with which you choose to do the monitoring. If you have to create a Visio diagram of your monitoring platform, it is too complicated.

The point of keeping your monitoring close to your infrastructure is meant to express that the tool used to monitor should physically reside close to the infrastructure/application. The monitoring platform should not have to traverse the VPNs or multiple firewalls just to poll the devices or applications. Centrally, you should place the monitoring platform so that you can poll as many systems as possible with minimal path to travel. You should be able to open up one or two ports in a firewall to enable monitoring and this should be turned into a standardized process part of deploying new devices or applications.

The last point is also a rather self-explanatory concept. Creating good monitors is critical and will avoid false positive monitor alerts. Over time, individuals will begin to ignore monitoring alerts if they all turn out to be false alarms. Make sure that each monitoring check works as expected and is tuned to avoid false alarms, as much as possible. You should never launch a new alert monitor without testing it during various workloads and at different times of the day. Also, it should go without saying to make sure that the monitor adds value and is not redundant.

Now that we have gotten the basics out of the way, we can now focus on monitoring OpenStack in the following four areas:

- Physical hardware (base resource consumption)
- OpenStack API endpoints
- OpenStack services processes
- Compute nodes via the infrastructure nodes

Since the first two areas are honestly better suited for a monitoring tool to handle, we will not be focusing on those tools in this book. So our focus will be primarily on checking the health of the infrastructure services (that is, Galera, RabbitMQ and so on), the core OpenStack services, processes and the compute nodes.

ProTip

When monitoring the OpenStack API endpoints, make sure to include the endpoint response time as a metric being recorded. This allows you to identify and track any service related slow-downs that eventually cause a service failure. Capturing this information allows you to see performance trends over time, which could proactively allow you to address service related issues before failures occur. The fix can be something as simple as adding more containers running that particular service, tuning service parameters, and/or database tuning.

OpenStack service processes

Before moving on to the next section, I felt it would be helpful to include some details on the OpenStack service processes. The following is a table outlining the OpenStack services and the associated process names. As with anything related to OpenStack, the process names are subject to change on a per-release basis, I am hoping that this will at least be a good starting point:

Service name	Code name	Process name
Compute	Nova	`nova-api-metadata, nova-api-os-compute, nova-cert, nova-compute, nova-consoleauth, nova-spicehtml5proxy, nova-api-ec2, nova-api, nova-conductor, nova-scheduler`
Object storage	Swift	`swift-proxy-server, swift-account-server, swift-account-auditor, swift-account-replicator, swift-account-reaper, swift-container-server, swift-container-auditor, swift-container-replicator, swift-container-updater, swift-object-server, swift-object-auditor, swift-object-replicator, swift-object-updater`
Image	Glance	`glance-api, glance-registry`
Identity	Keystone	`keystone-all, apache2`
Dashboard	Horizon	`apache2`

Service name	Code name	Process name
Networking	Neutron	`neutron-dhcp-agent`, `neutron-l3-agent`, `neutron-linuxbridge-agent`, `neutron-metadata-agent`, `neutron-metering-agent`, `neutron-server`
Block storage	Cinder	`cinder-api`, `cinder-volume`, `cinder-scheduler`
Orchestration	Heat	`heat-api`, `heat-api-cfn`, `heat-api-cloudwatch`, `heat-engine`
Telemetry	Ceilometer	`ceilometer-agent-compute`, `ceilometer-agent-central`, `ceilometer-agent-notification`, `ceilometer-collector`, `ceilometer-alarm-evaluator`, `ceilometer-alarm-notifier`, `ceilometer-api`
Database	Trove	`trove-api`, `trove-taskmanager`, `trove-conductor`

Infrastructure services

The base behind all the OpenStack services is known as the infrastructure services. These are the services/components needed just for OpenStack to work on any level. The components are an SQL database server software, database-clustering software, and messaging server software. In our specific case, these components in the same order will be: MariaDB, Galera, and RabbitMQ. Make sure that all of these components are healthy and working as expected. Each of these software packages has native commands to report on their health, so we are covered there. So, the challenge will then be to decide the best way to query for this information against clouds of various sizes. Imagine that you have a twenty-node control plane. You could either execute the health check command twenty times or just execute one command, using Ansible, to get the status back.

MariaDB and Galera

Starting with the first two components, there is a way to execute one command to do both, a MySQL check as well as check the health of the database cluster. If you remember, back in Chapter 2, *An Introduction to Ansible*, we covered the topic of *Dynamic inventory* and how OSA has pre-built the available dynamic inventory scripts that we can use to ease cloud management. We will utilize that capability here to streamline the process of checking on these infrastructure services.

It may be useful to have a quick reminder walk through of how to use the OSA dynamic inventory scripts with Ansible. From the root OSA deployment directory, you can use the defined group names to call the containers where the OpenStack services reside. Each OpenStack service and infrastructure component has a group defined within the dynamic inventory. Related to the specific task that we are working on currently, there is a group called `galera_container`. This group contains all the containers where MySQL and Galera are installed for the cloud. You can then substitute this group name for any host name that you will normally provide within the `hosts` file located inside the root directory of the playbook. Try executing the following command against your OSA cloud to reveal the details for your Galera containers:

```
$./inventory/dynamic_inventory.py | grepgalera
```

The output will look similar to this:

```
root@021579-deploy01:/opt/os-ansible-deployment/rpc_deployment# ./inventory/dynamic_inventory.py | grep galera
    "galera_all": {
        "galera"
        "infra1_galera_container-3f1f79fb": {
            "component": "galera",
            "container_name": "infra1_galera_container-3f1f79fb",
    "galera": {
        "infra1_galera_container-3f1f79fb"
    "galera_container": {
        "infra1_galera_container-3f1f79fb"
        "infra1_galera_container-3f1f79fb",
        "infra1_galera_container-3f1f79fb",
```

Note that the above example was collected against an **all-in-one** (**AIO**) deployment of OpenStack. Normally, you should find three or more different containers listed under the `galera_container` group.

One area that we have never covered as it relates to Ansible is the ability to issue more basic ad hoc commands using just the `ansible` runtime package. Execute the following command within a command prompt where Ansible is installed to see the details of how to use the basic Ansible program:

```
$ ansible -h
```

You will notice that the parameters are very similar to the `ansible-playbook` program, with the main difference being that the `ansible` program is not intended to execute playbooks. Rather, it is meant to be able to execute ad-hoc tasks directly on the command line using the same modules that you will normally use with a playbook. We will use the basic Ansible program to demonstrate how to retrieve the status of these infrastructure services.

Now, if we put this all together, the working example of reporting on the health of MySQL and Galera will look similar to the following:

```
$ ansible galera_container -m shell -a "mysql -h localhost\
 -e 'show status like \"%wsrep_cluster_%\";'"
```

The preceding command told Ansible to use the `galera_container` group as the host to run the shell command in the command line statement above. The `shell` command will call MySQL and execute the `show status` query. The output of the command will look similar to the following screenshot:

Again, due to using an AIO deployment, you will notice that the example shows a cluster size of only one. Normally, the cluster size should show three or more and the status will be displayed for each container (the output will be repeated for each container).The key areas to look out for are: each container reports `success`, the cluster size is correct, and the cluster ID is the same across all clusters.

RabbitMQ

We will use the same principles as we did earlier for MariaDB/Galera, to check on the status and health of the RabbitMQ cluster. The group name for the RabbitMQ containers is `rabbit_mq_container` and we can see the details of the group by executing the following command within the OSA root deployment directory:

```
$./inventory/dynamic_inventory.py | greprabbit_mq
```

We can now go ahead and test a few commands to report the RabbitMQ cluster health. The first command in the following code block will report directly on the cluster status and the second command will list out all the queues that contain messages (in other words, queues that are not empty):

```
$ ansible rabbit_mq_container -m shell -a "rabbitmqctl cluster_status"
ansible rabbit_mq_container -m shell -a "rabbitmqctl list_queues | awk '\$2>0'"
```

The output of the commands will look similar to the following screenshot:

```
root@021579-deploy01:/opt/os-ansible-deployment/rpc_deployment# ansible rabbit_mq_container -m shel
infra1_rabbit_mq_container-6193dd22 | success | rc=0 >>
Cluster status of node 'rabbit@infra1_rabbit_mq_container-6193dd22' ...
[{nodes,[{disc,['rabbit@infra1_rabbit_mq_container-6193dd22']}]},
 {running_nodes,['rabbit@infra1_rabbit_mq_container-6193dd22']},
 {cluster_name,<<"rpc">>},
 {partitions,[]}]

root@021579-deploy01:/opt/os-ansible-deployment/rpc_deployment# ansible rabbit_mq_container -m shel
infra1_rabbit_mq_container-6193dd22 | success | rc=0 >>
Listing queues ...
notifications.info        34
```

Having each container report back a `success`, having the list of running nodes match exactly, and each showing the same cluster name are the areas that matter the most. Do not stress too much if you find queues with messages still present. The idea is that the messages should clear in an acceptable period of time. Use this metric to seek out any trends in messages that are getting stuck in the queue for too long.

Core OpenStack services

With all the infrastructure services covered, we can move on to the core OpenStack services. In this section, we will cover a few principles that can be used for any of the OpenStack services. This approach allows you to interchange any of the basic approaches for any service, based on your personal needs.

The first three services that I normally go in and check are Keystone, Nova, and Neutron. These services can have adverse effects on many other services within your cloud and need to be running properly to technically have a functioning cloud. While there is no distinct OpenStack command that you can use to check the Keystone service, it will become very obvious if the Keystone service is not operational, as any/all OpenStack CLI commands will fail. I personally feel that the easiest way to test our Keystone is to either log into the Horizon dashboard or issue the following Keystone CLI command:

```
$ keystone service-list
```

If you get the list of services using Keystone, you have just tested the passing of user credentials to Keystone for authentication and Keystone returned back a proper token for the authorization. With us taking care of testing our own Keystone, the next step can be to issue two OpenStack CLI commands that will quickly report on the state of Nova and Neutron:

```
$ nova service-list
```

```
$ neutron agent-list
```

The `nova service-list` command will poll all Nova related containers and compute nodes to determine their zone, status, state, and the date/time of the last update. The output of this command will look similar to this:

Next, the `neutron agent-list` command will do the same thing as the preceding example, except for the Neutron related components. You will notice that in the following example, a smiley face graphic is used to determine the status of the Neutron agents. The state of the agents will also be reported back with this. Below is an example of the output of the neutron agent-list command:

At this point, you will have to rely on checking directly on the statuses of the actual OpenStack service processes running within their containers to do a more detailed monitoring. This will be similar to some of the methods published on the OpenStack website at `http://docs.openstack.org/openstack-ops/content/logging_ monitoring.html#monitoring`. The main difference is the fact that we will be able to use Ansible to execute the commands across all the containers or nodes as needed. Using the preceding basic Ansible program and the OpenStack service processes table, you will be able to check the status of the processes running OpenStack within your cloud. The following are a few examples of how this can be accomplished. It is recommended that you get a complete output of the dynamic inventory for your cloud, so you will be aware of all the groups defined. Use the following command to get the complete inventory output (this command assumes that you are in the root OSA deployment directory):

```
$ cd playbooks/inventory
$ ./dynamic_inventory.py
```

You will have to save the JSON output where you can refer to it in the future.

Service and process check examples

The following are a few examples of how you can execute service and process monitor checks using Ansible:

```
# check if a process is running
$ ansible neutron_server_container -m shell -a "ps -ef | grep neutron-
server"


# check status of a service
$ ansible compute_hosts -m shell -a "service nova-compute status"


# stop/start/restart a service (process)
$ ansible glance_container -m shell -a "service glance-registry stop"
$ ansible glance_container -m shell -a "service glance-registry start"
$ ansible glance_container -m shell -a "service glance-registry restart"


# parseservice logs
$ ansible nova_scheduler_container -m shell -a "grep 35f83ac8 /var/log/
nova/nova-scheduler.log"
```

You can use any of these examples to determine the health of your OpenStack services on a cloud of any size, big or small. Imagine the power of being able to query the `nova-compute` service status across a cloud with 200 nodes in one command. Good stuff, right? Well, of course we have to try to take it to the next level in the next section by having some of these health checks delivered right to your inbox, at an interval of your choice.

Coding the playbook and roles

In this section, we will now create the playbook and roles to generate our cloud health report. Once the playbook is executed, the output and end result will be a single report with some of the monitoring checks that we reviewed in the previous section. Just as shown in the last chapter, the report can be saved into a directory of your choice. This time around, we have broken up the tasks into three roles in order to keep things simple. Let's review each role in the following sections:

cloud-infra-check

The first role that we will create will include the tasks needed to set up the foundation for the cloud health report. The name of the file will be `main.yml` located within the role directory named `cloud-infra-check/tasks`. The contents of this file will look similar to this:

```
---
- name: Create working directory
shell: mkdir {{ REPORT_DIR }}
ignore_errors: yes

- name: Copy the Infrastructure services check script
template: src=infra_check.sh dest={{ DEPLOY_LOC }} mode=0755

- name: Add report header
shell: ( echo "+--------------------------------------+"; echo "|
{{ COMPANY }} Cloud Health Check    |"; echo "| Created at {{
lookup('pipe', 'date +%Y-%m-%d%t%X') }}   |"; echo "+------------------
------------------+"; echo " ";) >> {{ REPORT_DIR }}/os_health_check_
{{ lookup('pipe', 'date +%Y%m%d') }}.txt

- name: Execute Infrastructure services check script
shell: "'{{ DEPLOY_LOC }}/infra_check.sh' {{ REPORT_DIR }}"
```

The first three tasks are simply handling the prerequisite steps needed to create the report. This will include creating the directory where the report is saved, copying the shell script to be executed, and adding the header to the report. We will use some of the formatting created in the last chapters report here also.

The final task will execute the `infra_check.sh`, which will handle the infrastructure services checks from the OSA deployment node. The `infra_check.sh` script will be stored in the `cloud-infra-check/templates` directory of this role. This is so that we can leverage the variables defined in your playbook already, instead of hard coding directory paths and so on. The contents of the file will look similar to this:

```
#
# Script to automate OpenStack cloud Infrastructure services health
check
#
NOW=$(date +"%Y%m%d")

# Check health of MariaDB and Galera
ansible -i {{ DEPLOY_LOC }}/inventory/dynamic_inventory.py galera_
container -m shell -a "mysql -h localhost -e 'show status like
\"%wsrep_cluster_%\";'" >> {{ REPORT_DIR }}/os_health_check_$NOW.txt

# Check health of RabbitMQ
ansible -i {{ DEPLOY_LOC }}/inventory/dynamic_inventory.py rabbit_mq_
container -m shell -a "rabbitmqctl cluster_status" >> {{ REPORT_DIR
}}/os_health_check_$NOW.txt

# Check queue health of RabbitMQ
ansible -i {{ DEPLOY_LOC }}/inventory/dynamic_inventory.py rabbit_mq_
container -m shell -a "rabbitmqctl list_queues | awk '\$2>0'" >> {{
REPORT_DIR }}/os_health_check_$NOW.txt

exit 0
```

You will notice that we are using the basic Ansible ad-hoc commands to gather the status for the infrastructure components; as well as utilizing the dynamic inventory script included with your OSA deployment.

cloud-core-os-check

The next role will focus on handling native OpenStack CLI commands that can be used to determine the health of your cloud. The file will be named `main.yml` located within the role directory name `cloud-core-os-check/tasks`. The contents of this file will look similar this:

```
---
- name: Create working directory
shell: mkdir {{ REPORT_DIR }}
ignore_errors: yes

- name: Verify Keystone functionality
shell: ( keystone --os-username={{ OS_USERNAME }} --os-password={{
OS_PASSWORD }} --os-tenant-name={{ OS_TENANT_NAME }} --os-auth-url={{
OS_AUTH_URL }}
service-list && echo " " ) >> {{ REPORT_DIR }}/core_os_check_{{
lookup('pipe', 'date +%Y%m%d') }}.txt
ignore_errors: yes

- name: Verify Nova functionality
shell: ( nova --os-username={{ OS_USERNAME }} --os-password={{ OS_
PASSWORD }} --os-tenant-name={{ OS_TENANT_NAME }} --os-auth-url={{
OS_AUTH_URL }}
service-list && echo " " ) >> {{ REPORT_DIR }}/core_os_check_{{
lookup('pipe', 'date +%Y%m%d') }}.txt
ignore_errors: yes

- name: Verify Neutron functionality
shell: ( neutron --os-username={{ OS_USERNAME }} --os-password={{
OS_PASSWORD }} --os-tenant-name={{ OS_TENANT_NAME }} --os-auth-url={{
OS_AUTH_URL }}
agent-list && echo " " ) >> {{ REPORT_DIR }}/core_os_check_{{
lookup('pipe', 'date +%Y%m%d') }}.txt
ignore_errors: yes

- name: Retrieve core OS output file
fetch: src={{ REPORT_DIR }}/core_os_check_{{ lookup('pipe', 'date
+%Y%m%d') }}.txt dest={{ REPORT_DEST }} flat=yes
```

All the pre-setup work for the report is being handled in the preceding first task (creating the report directory). The three commands used here are: `keystone service-list`, `nova service-list`, and `neutron agent-list`. These are the same commands discussed in the core OpenStack services section earlier in this chapter. The output of these commands is saved into a text file that will be merged together with the other outputs collected. The last task in this role will go retrieve it from the report from the remote location and move it locally to where the playbook/roles are executed.

os-service-status

This role will be responsible for inspecting the service status for the provided OpenStack services as an added bonus. The file will be named `main.yml` within the role directory name `os-service-status/tasks`. In the following example, you will find the contents of this file:

```
---
- name: Combine Infrastructure and Core OS output
shell: cat {{ REPORT_DEST }}/core_os_check_{{ lookup('pipe', 'date
+%Y%m%d') }}.txt >> {{ REPORT_DIR }}/os_health_check_{{ lookup('pipe',
'date +%Y%m%d') }}.txt

- name: Check OS service status
shell: ansible -i {{ DEPLOY_LOC }}/inventory/dynamic_inventory.py  {{
item.0.name }} -m shell
        -a "service {{ item.1 }} status" >> {{ REPORT_DIR }}/os_
health_check_{{ lookup('pipe', 'date +%Y%m%d') }}.txt
with_subelements:
    - os_group
    - process
```

The last role consists of the two last tasks. The first task will take care of merging the two report outputs into one file and the second task will perform the service status checks, based on the input provided in the variable file associated with this role. This role is modular in the sense that you can add or remove as many services to check as you want. We will review this variable file in more detail in the following section. A small unique feature with this role is the fact that we will use basic Ansible ad-hoc commands inside a playbook. By doing this, we simplify the playbook complexity to be able to use the dynamic inventory just for this specific task.

To support these roles, we now need to create the variable files that will go along with it. Since we will use two separate hosts to execute the series of roles against, there will be two global variable files needed and one local variable file for one of the roles. The file names are `util_container` and `localhost`, they will be saved to the `group_vars/` directory of the playbook. The local variable file is associated with the `os-service-status` role and can be found in the `os-service-status/vars` directory.

Note that the values defined in the variable file are intended to be changed before each execution for normal everyday use.

No new variables were added to the `util_container` variable file from the last chapter. However, the `localhost` variable file is a new file and has new variables defined. Since two of the three roles will use the local host to run a part of the playbook, we had to add some of the variables already defined in the `util_container` file. The contents of this new file are, as shown:

```
# Here are variables related globally to the localhost

REPORT_DIR: /usr/share/os-report
COMPANY: Rackspace RPC
DEPLOY_LOC: /opt/os-ansible-deployment/rpc_deployment
REPORT_DEST: /usr/share/
```

The local variable file named `main.yml`, associated with the `os-service-status` role, will be where you can define the dynamic inventory groups and OpenStack services that you will check the status of. See the working example of the contents of this file, as shown:

```
---
os_group:
  - name: keystone_container
process:
      - apache2
  - name: compute_hosts
process:
      - nova-compute
      - neutron-linuxbridge-agent
  - name: nova_api_os_compute_container
process:
      - nova-api-os-compute
  - name: nova_scheduler_container
process:
      - nova-scheduler
  - name: neutron_server_container
process:
      - neutron-server
  - name: neutron_linuxbridge_agent
process:
      - neutron-linuxbridge-agent
  - name: glance_container
process:
      - glance-api
      - glance-registry
  - name: horizon_container
process:
      - apache2
```

Let's take a moment to break down the new variables. The summary will be:

```
REPORT_DIR  # the directory where the report is stored temporarily
remotely

REPORT_DEST  # the directory where the report is saved locally

DEPLOY_LOC  # the root OSA deployment directory

COMPANY   # the company name to show up in the report header


os_group
   name    # name of the dynamic inventory group
   process # name of the OS service process
```

 Since there are two global variable files that share the same variable names, please make sure to keep the variable value in sync if you want both reports in the same directory.

With the variable file completed, we can move on to creating the master playbook file. Since we created three roles to handle the collection of the health of the cloud and will utilize two different hosts, we can use the following approach to execute the roles from one playbook. The complete contents of the playbook file will end up looking similar to this:

```
---
# This playbook used to run a cloud health check report.

- hosts: localhost
user: root
remote_user: root
sudo: yes
roles:
    - cloud-infra-check

- hosts: util_container
user: root
remote_user: root
sudo: yes
roles:
    - cloud-core-os-check
```

```
  - hosts: localhost
user: root
remote_user: root
sudo: yes
roles:
    - os-service-status
```

The roles we created will be executed in the order displayed in the playbook. Note that the local host (`localhost`) in this example is the node used to deploy OSA.

> The playbook and role names can be anything you choose. Specific names have been provided here in order to allow you to easily follow along and reference the completed code found in the GitHub repository. The only warning is, whatever you decide to name them, the roles must remain uniform when referenced from within the playbook(s).

Nothing new needs to be added to the inventory file since we already had `localhost` and the `util_container`. I hope you are happy with how it all came out. In keeping with our tradition, we will finish the chapter with a quick review of the playbook and role just created.

Playbook and role review

Let's jump right into examining the roles we created.

The completed role and file named `main.yml` located in the `cloud-infra-check/tasks` directory looks similar to this:

```
---
- name: Create working directory
shell: mkdir {{ REPORT_DIR }}
ignore_errors: yes

- name: Copy the Infrastructure services check script
template: src=infra_check.sh dest={{ DEPLOY_LOC }} mode=0755

- name: Add report header
shell: ( echo "+-------------------------------------+"; echo "|
{{ COMPANY }} Cloud Health Check    |"; echo "| Created at {{
lookup('pipe', 'date +%Y-%m-%d%t%X') }}  |"; echo "+------------------
------------------+"; echo " ";) >> {{ REPORT_DIR }}/os_health_check_
{{ lookup('pipe', 'date +%Y%m%d') }}.txt

- name: Execute Infrastructure services check script
shell: "'{{ DEPLOY_LOC }}/infra_check.sh' {{ REPORT_DIR }}"
```

The completed role and file named `main.yml` located in the `cloud-core-os-check/` `tasks` directory is as shown:

```
---
- name: Create working directory
  shell: mkdir {{ REPORT_DIR }}
  ignore_errors: yes


- name: Verify Keystone functionality
  shell: ( keystone --os-username={{ OS_USERNAME }} --os-password={{
OS_PASSWORD }} --os-tenant-name={{ OS_TENANT_NAME }} --os-auth-url={{
OS_AUTH_URL }}
service-list && echo " " ) >> {{ REPORT_DIR }}/core_os_check_{{
lookup('pipe', 'date +%Y%m%d') }}.txt
  ignore_errors: yes


- name: Verify Nova functionality
  shell: ( nova --os-username={{ OS_USERNAME }} --os-password={{ OS_
PASSWORD }} --os-tenant-name={{ OS_TENANT_NAME }} --os-auth-url={{
OS_AUTH_URL }}
service-list && echo " " ) >> {{ REPORT_DIR }}/core_os_check_{{
lookup('pipe', 'date +%Y%m%d') }}.txt
  ignore_errors: yes


- name: Verify Neutron functionality
  shell: ( neutron --os-username={{ OS_USERNAME }} --os-password={{
OS_PASSWORD }} --os-tenant-name={{ OS_TENANT_NAME }} --os-auth-url={{
OS_AUTH_URL }}
agent-list && echo " " ) >> {{ REPORT_DIR }}/core_os_check_{{
lookup('pipe', 'date +%Y%m%d') }}.txt
  ignore_errors: yes


- name: Retrieve core OS output file
  fetch: src={{ REPORT_DIR }}/core_os_check_{{ lookup('pipe', 'date
+%Y%m%d') }}.txt dest={{ REPORT_DEST }} flat=yes
```

The completed role and file named `main.yml` located in the `os-service-status/` `tasks` directory looks similar to this:

```
---
- name: Combine Infrastructure and Core OS output
  shell: cat {{ REPORT_DEST }}/core_os_check_{{ lookup('pipe', 'date
+%Y%m%d') }}.txt >> {{ REPORT_DIR }}/os_health_check_{{ lookup('pipe',
'date +%Y%m%d') }}.txt
```

```
- name: Check OS service status
shell: ansible -i {{ DEPLOY_LOC }}/inventory/dynamic_inventory.py  {{
item.0.name }} -m shell
         -a "service {{ item.1 }} status" >> {{ REPORT_DIR }}/os_
health_check_{{ lookup('pipe', 'date +%Y%m%d') }}.txt
with_subelements:
    - os_group
    - process
```

The corresponding global variable file is named `util_container` and is saved to the `group_vars/` directory of the complete playbook:

```
# Here are variables related globally to the util_container host group

OS_USERNAME: admin
OS_PASSWORD: passwd
OS_TENANT_NAME: admin
OS_AUTH_URL: http://172.29.236.7:35357/v2.0
REPORT_DIR: /usr/share/os-report
REPORT_DEST: /usr/share/
RPTSTART: 2015-09-01
RPTEND: 2015-10-03
```

The corresponding global variable file is named `localhost` and is saved to the `group_vars/` directory of the complete playbook:

```
# Here are variables related globally to the localhost

REPORT_DIR: /usr/share/os-report
COMPANY: Rackspace RPC
DEPLOY_LOC: /opt/os-ansible-deployment/rpc_deployment
REPORT_DEST: /usr/share/
```

The corresponding local variable file named `main.yml` and is located in the `os-service-status/vars` directory of the `os-service-status` role:

```
---
os_group:
  - name: keystone_container
process:
      - apache2
  - name: compute_hosts
process:
      - nova-compute
      - neutron-linuxbridge-agent
  - name: nova_api_os_compute_container
```

```
process:
        - nova-api-os-compute
  - name: nova_scheduler_container
process:
        - nova-scheduler
  - name: neutron_server_container
process:
        - neutron-server
  - name: neutron_linuxbridge_agent
process:
        - neutron-linuxbridge-agent
  - name: glance_container
process:
        - glance-api
        - glance-registry
  - name: horizon_container
process:
        - apache2
```

Now, the master playbook file was created and will be located in the root of the playbook directory.

The `health-check.yml` file will look as follows:

```
---
# This playbook used to run a cloud health check report.

- hosts: localhost
user: root
remote_user: root
sudo: yes
roles:
    - cloud-infra-check

- hosts: util_container
user: root
remote_user: root
sudo: yes
roles:
    - cloud-core-os-check

- hosts: localhost
user: root
remote_user: root
sudo: yes
roles:
    - os-service-status
```

Finally, at the end we created the `hosts` file, which is also located in the root of the playbook directory:

```
[localhost]
localhost ansible_connection=local

[util_container]
172.29.236.85
```

The complete set of code can be found in the following GitHub repository: `https://github.com/os-admin-with-ansible/os-admin-with-ansible/tree/master/cloud-health-check`.

Before we finish this topic, we need to test out our work. At the end of running this playbook and role, you will have a quick cloud health report to review. Assuming that you have cloned the preceding GitHub repository, the command to test out the playbook from the `Deployment` node will be as follows:

```
$ cd os-admin-with-ansible/cloud-health-check
$ ansible-playbook -i hosts health-check.yml
```

Assuming that the playbook ran successfully and completed with no errors, you should find a single report created in the directory you specified in the global variable file. The first section of the report should look similar to the following screenshot:

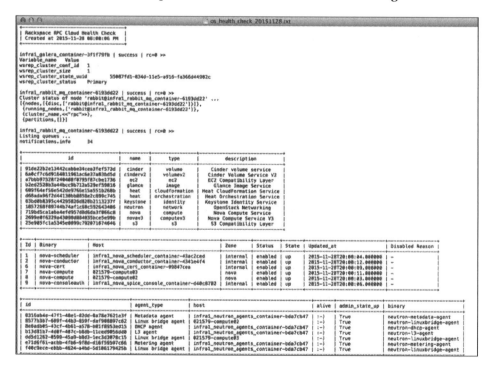

A screenshot of the second section of the report, which includes the status of the OpenStack processes is included below.

```
infra1_keystone_container-15b80c4e | success | rc=0 >>
 * apache2 is running

compute3 | success | rc=0 >>
nova-compute start/running, process 970

compute1 | success | rc=0 >>
nova-compute start/running, process 5607

compute2 | success | rc=0 >>
nova-compute start/running, process 970

compute1 | success | rc=0 >>
neutron-linuxbridge-agent start/running, process 12343

compute3 | success | rc=0 >>
neutron-linuxbridge-agent start/running, process 6613

compute2 | success | rc=0 >>
neutron-linuxbridge-agent start/running, process 6613

infra1_nova_api_os_compute_container-7294f6e6 | success | rc=0 >>
nova-api-os-compute start/running, process 2425

infra1_nova_scheduler_container-43ac2ced | success | rc=0 >>
nova-scheduler start/running, process 2224

infra1_neutron_server_container-77ce2829 | success | rc=0 >>
neutron-server start/running, process 1806

compute1 | success | rc=0 >>
neutron-linuxbridge-agent start/running, process 12343

compute2 | success | rc=0 >>
neutron-linuxbridge-agent start/running, process 6613

compute3 | success | rc=0 >>
neutron-linuxbridge-agent start/running, process 6613

infra1_neutron_agents_container-bda7cb47 | success | rc=0 >>
neutron-linuxbridge-agent start/running, process 932
```

Summary

Here we are again, with yet another tool to add to our OpenStack administration toolbox. Having a quick cloud health report at your fingertips is extremely useful and valuable. Remember, this is only a starting point. I expect you to improve/customize it for your specific needs. I am looking forward to seeing all your great work in the future. Before wrapping up this final chapter, let's take a moment to recap. Together we reviewed some monitoring tips and tricks and examined the OpenStack components worth monitoring. Next, we learned how to use Ansible ad-hoc commands. Lastly, we developed an Ansible playbook and role to automate the generation of cloud reports.

Well ladies and gentleman, it has been fun and honestly a privilege to be allowed to share these automation examples with you. Do keep up the great work and also keep an eye out for future revisions as both OpenStack and Ansible continues to mature. I'm really looking forward to hearing your feedback and seeing how you took these examples to the next level.

Index

R

RabbitMQ 174, 175
Raksha
  reference 62
role-based access controls (RBAC) 4
roles 19, 20

S

Secure Shell (SSH) 16
snapshots
  creating manually 63-65
  defining 61-63

T

tenant access
  assigning 31
tenant configuration steps, multi-tenant
    isolation
  about 100
  custom flavor, creating 102, 103
  existing tenant, using 100
  host aggregate metadata, updating 102
  hosts, adding to new host aggregate 101
  new host aggregate, creating 100
  tenant, creating 100
  volume type quotas, applying 103, 104
tenant-inventory 156
tenant report 146
tenants
  creating 29-31
  creating manually 30

U

user-inventory 155, 156
user report 144
users
  creating 29, 30
  creating manually 30
users role
  assigning 31

V

variables
  about 22
  registering 23
  variable placeholders, setting 22
  variable values, setting 22
volume-inventory 157-160
volume report 149, 150

W

working examples
  about 9
  endpoints, listing 9
  services, listing 9

Thank you for buying
OpenStack Administration with Ansible

About Packt Publishing

Packt, pronounced 'packed', published its first book, *Mastering phpMyAdmin for Effective MySQL Management*, in April 2004, and subsequently continued to specialize in publishing highly focused books on specific technologies and solutions.

Our books and publications share the experiences of your fellow IT professionals in adapting and customizing today's systems, applications, and frameworks. Our solution-based books give you the knowledge and power to customize the software and technologies you're using to get the job done. Packt books are more specific and less general than the IT books you have seen in the past. Our unique business model allows us to bring you more focused information, giving you more of what you need to know, and less of what you don't.

Packt is a modern yet unique publishing company that focuses on producing quality, cutting-edge books for communities of developers, administrators, and newbies alike. For more information, please visit our website at www.packtpub.com.

About Packt Open Source

In 2010, Packt launched two new brands, Packt Open Source and Packt Enterprise, in order to continue its focus on specialization. This book is part of the Packt Open Source brand, home to books published on software built around open source licenses, and offering information to anybody from advanced developers to budding web designers. The Open Source brand also runs Packt's Open Source Royalty Scheme, by which Packt gives a royalty to each open source project about whose software a book is sold.

Writing for Packt

We welcome all inquiries from people who are interested in authoring. Book proposals should be sent to author@packtpub.com. If your book idea is still at an early stage and you would like to discuss it first before writing a formal book proposal, then please contact us; one of our commissioning editors will get in touch with you.

We're not just looking for published authors; if you have strong technical skills but no writing experience, our experienced editors can help you develop a writing career, or simply get some additional reward for your expertise.

open source
community experience distilled

Learning OpenStack

ISBN: 978-1-78398-696-5   Paperback: 272 pages

Set up and maintain your own cloud-based
Infrastructure as a Service (IaaS) using OpenStack

1. Build and manage a cloud environment using
    just four virtual machines.

2. Get to grips with mandatory as well as optional
    OpenStack components and know how they
    work together.

3. Leverage your cloud environment to provide
    Infrastructure as a Service (IaaS) with this
    practical, step-by-step guide.

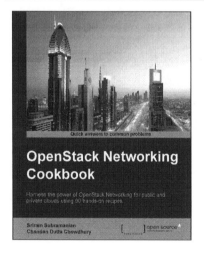

OpenStack Networking Cookbook

ISBN: 978-1-78528-610-0   Paperback: 282 pages

Harness the power of OpenStack Networking for
public and private clouds using 90 hands-on recipes

1. Build and manage virtual switching, routing,
    and firewall-based networks in OpenStack
    using Neutron.

2. Develop plugins and drivers for Neutron to
    enhance the built-in networking capabilities.

3. Monitor and automate OpenStack networks
    using tools like Ceilometer and Heat.

Please check **www.PacktPub.com** for information on our titles

Learning OpenStack High Availability

ISBN: 978-1-78439-570-4   Paperback: 156 pages

Build a resilient and scalable OpenStack cloud, using advanced open source tools

1. Leverage the power of OpenStack to achieve high availability.

2. Get to grips with concepts such as Galeria Cluster for Glance and Cinder, MariaDB, and validation.

3. Using clustering and high-availability solutions, this book provides a comprehensive plan for you to connect them with Red Hat Enterprise Linux OpenStack Platform.

Mastering Ansible

ISBN: 978-1-78439-548-3   Paperback: 236 pages

Design, develop, and solve real world automation and orchestration needs by unlocking the automation capabilities of Ansible

1. Discover how Ansible works in detail.

2. Explore use cases for Ansible's advanced features including task delegation, fast failures, and serial task execution.

3. Extend Ansible with custom modules, plugins, and inventory sources.

Please check **www.PacktPub.com** for information on our titles

Made in the USA
Lexington, KY
23 April 2016